Artistry of Eldercare: A Guide For Adult Children of Aging Parents

Walt Kasmir, PhD

Published by Atum Dunamis Press, 2024.

While every precaution has been taken in the preparation of this book, the publisher assumes no responsibility for errors or omissions, or for damages resulting from the use of the information contained herein.

ARTISTRY OF ELDERCARE: A GUIDE FOR ADULT CHILDREN OF AGING PARENTS

Table of Contents

My wife, Valerie, has been the guiding light, the unwavering muse, and the inspiration behind every word penned. Your love, support, and unwavering belief in me have shaped this journey into something beautiful.

This book is a testament to the endless inspiration you bring into my life. Thank you for being my muse, my confidante, and my forever love.

Preface

Welcome to *Artistry of Eldercare: A Guide For Adult Children of Aging Parents*, a book born out of my understanding that eldercare is much more than a series of tasks and responsibilities.

In the pages that follow, you won't find a one-size-fits-all approach. Instead, I acknowledge that the journey of caring for aging parents is deeply personal and varied. Like any art, eldercare requires us to adapt advice and strategies to you our own temperament, skills, and experiences, as well as to the unique personalities and needs of your parents. It's a journey of continuous learning, improvisation, and, most importantly, love. This book is structured to guide you through this complex and rewarding journey.

Each chapter is crafted to provide insight into the various aspects of eldercare, from understanding the global aging landscape and navigating legal and ethical considerations to managing care remotely, and making the home a safe, nurturing environment for aging in place. Real-life scenarios and case studies are woven throughout to offer practical examples and to illustrate the artistry required in adapting these strategies to your personal situation.

Eldercare, much like art, thrives on creativity and empathy. It involves painting a picture of comfort and care that resonates with the unique hues of your family's history, values, and dynamics. It's about composing a symphony of support that harmonizes the needs, fears, and aspirations of your aging loved ones with your own capabilities and circumstances. As you turn these pages, I invite you to embrace the artistry in your role as a caregiver.

Blessings,
Walt Kasmir, PhD, RN, BCPC

Self-Care Introduction

Executive Summary

In the intricate experience of eldercare, the well-being of the caregiver holds equal importance to that of the care receiver. This chapter delves into the often-overlooked realm of ACAP self-care, acknowledging the immense stress and potential health risks associated with the caregiving role. With a compassionate lens, we explore proactive strategies designed not only to preserve the health and well-being of caregivers but also to enhance their capacity to provide compassionate care.

As we navigate through these pages, we aim to empower Adult Children of Aging Parents with the tools and insights necessary to sustain their own health and vitality alongside that of their loved ones.

Key Points

1. **Acknowledging the Stress of Caregiving**. Understanding the multifaceted nature of caregiver stress and its implications on physical and emotional health.
2. **Health Risks for Caregivers**. Identifying the potential health risks associated with prolonged stress and emotional strain, including burnout, depression, and physical health decline.
3. **Proactive Self-Care Strategies**. Outlining essential self-care practices that can mitigate the impact of caregiving stress, promote well-being, and prevent caregiver burnout.
4. **Creating a Support Network**. Emphasizing the importance of building a robust support system, including family, friends, community resources, and professional support.
5. **Balancing Caregiving with Personal Needs**. Strategies for maintaining personal health, interests, and relationships while fulfilling the caregiving role.

Learning Objectives

- **Recognize the Signs of Caregiver Stress**. Equip caregivers with the ability to identify early signs of stress and burnout in themselves, fostering a proactive approach to managing their well-being.
- **Understand the Importance of Self-Care**. Highlight the critical role of self-care in the caregiving journey, encouraging caregivers to prioritize their own health and happiness as integral to effective caregiving.
- **Implement Effective Self-Care Practices**. Provide caregivers with practical and effective self-care strategies that can be seamlessly integrated into their daily routines, ensuring their resilience and well-being.
- **Cultivate a Supportive Caregiving Environment**. Guide caregivers in building and utilizing a support network, reducing the isolation often felt in the caregiving role and promoting a sense of community and shared responsibility.

- **Achieve a Balanced Life**. Empower caregivers to find a balance between their caregiving responsibilities and personal needs, ensuring they can enjoy a fulfilling life while providing compassionate care.

As we embark on this crucial conversation about caregiver self-care, it's my hope that ACAPs will find solace, strength, and practical advice within these pages.

Self-Care:

The Art of Self-Care for Adult Children of Aging Parents (ACAPs)

Caring for an aging parent is a journey marked by profound love, dedication, and, inevitably, significant stress. For Adult Children of Aging Parents (ACAPs), the caregiving role often arrives intertwined with other life responsibilities, including managing their own family, career, and personal health.

This chapter delves into the essential yet often overlooked aspect of caregiving—the well-being of the caregiver. Recognizing the stress, potential health risks, and the crucial need for proactive self-care strategies is not just beneficial—it's imperative for sustaining the caregiving relationship over time.

Acknowledging the Stress of Caregiving

Caregiving, by its nature, is an all-consuming role that extends beyond physical tasks to emotional and financial support. The constant concern for your loved one's well-being, coupled with the fear of making critical decisions, can lead to overwhelming stress. This emotional toll is often compounded by the physical demands of caregiving, such as assisting with daily activities and managing medical needs. Recognizing this stress is the first step toward managing its impact. It's crucial to understand that feeling overwhelmed does not signify failure; rather, it's a common experience shared by caregivers across the globe.

Health Risks for Caregivers

The prolonged stress experienced by many ACAPs can lead to significant health risks, including anxiety, depression, and physical illness. Studies have shown that caregivers often put their own health needs on the back burner, leading to neglected chronic conditions and missed preventive care.

Burnout—a state of physical, emotional, and mental exhaustion—can also manifest, making caregivers susceptible to a decline in their ability to provide care. Acknowledging these risks is vital in prioritizing your health alongside your caregiving duties.

Proactive Self-Care Strategies

In the landscape of caregiving, where the well-being of another becomes your priority, it's all too easy to place your own needs on the back burner. However, embracing proactive self-care strategies is not just essential for maintaining your health; it's fundamental to ensuring you can continue to provide care effectively. Let's explore these strategies in more detail, emphasizing their importance in the caregiving journey.

The first pillar of proactive self-care involves staying vigilant about your own health needs through regular medical check-ups and screenings. This vigilance is crucial, as caregivers are often so absorbed in their caregiving duties that they neglect their health concerns until they become unavoidable. Scheduling and attending these appointments is a practical step in preventative care, helping to catch and manage potential health issues early on. Remember, ensuring your health is in check is not selfish; it's necessary for both you and those you care for.

Incorporating mindfulness and meditation into your daily routine can significantly mitigate the stress that comes with caregiving. These practices encourage a moment-to-moment awareness of our thoughts, feelings, bodily sensations, and surrounding environment, promoting a state of calmness and balance. Even a few minutes a day can help clear your mind, reduce stress, and improve your emotional equilibrium. Whether it's through guided meditation apps, prayer, or simply spending a few quiet moments in nature, mindfulness practices can be a sanctuary of peace in the chaos of caregiving.

Regular physical activity is another cornerstone of self-care. Exercise releases endorphins, often referred to as the body's natural stress relievers and mood lifters. Whether it's a brisk walk in the park, a yoga session, or a workout at the gym, finding an activity that you enjoy and can engage in regularly is key. Physical activity not only helps manage stress and improve your mood but also supports overall physical health, providing you with the energy strength needed for caregiving

Nourishing your body with a balanced and nutritious diet is essential for maintaining the energy levels required for caregiving. A diet rich in fruits, vegetables, lean proteins, and whole grains can boost your immune system, increase your energy, and help you maintain a healthy weight. While the demands of caregiving might tempt you to opt for quick and convenient meals, prioritizing nutrition can have a profound impact on your overall well-being. Finally, never underestimate the importance of rest and sleep. Caregivers often experience disrupted sleep patterns, either due to the demands of caregiving or the stress and anxiety that accompany their role. Prioritizing sleep is crucial for your body to repair and rejuvenate. Creating a bedtime routine, ensuring a comfortable sleep environment, and addressing any sleep issues are vital steps towards ensuring you get the rest you need.

By integrating these proactive self-care strategies into your life, you can create a foundation of well-being that supports both you and your caregiving journey. Self-care is the fuel that enables you to care for others with compassion, energy, and resilience. Remember, in the art of caregiving, caring for yourself is not an act of self-indulgence but an act of self-preservation and a profound expression of love.

Creating a Support Network

No caregiver should have to navigate their journey alone. Building a support network of family, friends, community resources, and professional services can provide the emotional and practical support needed. Support groups, both in-person and online, offer a space to share experiences and strategies with those in similar situations, reducing feelings of isolation.

Balancing Caregiving with Personal Needs

Balancing caregiving with personal needs requires setting boundaries, accepting help, and maintaining personal interests. It's important to:

- **Set Realistic Goals. Recognize** what you can and cannot do. Setting realistic goals can help manage the expectations of both you and your loved one.
- **Delegate Tasks.** Don't hesitate to delegate tasks to other family members or seek professional help for caregiving duties.
- **Preserve Personal Time.** Ensure you set aside time for activities that bring you joy and relaxation, away from your caregiving responsibilities.

Conclusion

For ACAPs, self-care is not a luxury—it's a necessity. Nurturing your own well-being enables you to provide the best care for your aging loved one. Remember, caring for yourself is an act of love, a critical component of the caregiving journey that empowers you to continue with strength, compassion, and resilience.

By adopting proactive self-care strategies and seeking the support you need, you can navigate the challenges of caregiving while maintaining your health and well-being.

Let this chapter be a reminder and a guide: in the art of caregiving, the caregiver's well-being is paramount, a truth that, once embraced.

Overview of Part I

Executive Summary

Part I serves as the foundational layer for your journey into eldercare. This section aims to provide you with a holistic understanding of the various facets that make up the complex world of caring for aging parents.

Key Points

1. The Aging Population: A Global Perspective

Here, we delve into the demographics and trends that are shaping the aging population globally. This sets the stage for understanding the scale and urgency of the eldercare issue.

2. The Emotional Quotient: Balancing Love and Responsibility

Eldercare is not just a logistical challenge but an emotional one. This chapter helps you navigate the emotional complexities involved in caring for an aging parent.

3. Legal and Ethical Considerations

From power of attorney to living wills, this chapter outlines the legal frameworks you need to be aware of.

4. Financial Planning for Eldercare

Finances can be a significant stressor in eldercare. This chapter provides a roadmap for budgeting, understanding insurance, and protecting against financial scams targeting the elderly.

Learning Objectives

- Gain a comprehensive understanding of the global aging population and its impact on families.
- Develop emotional intelligence skills specific to the challenges of eldercare.
- Acquire knowledge about the legal and ethical frameworks that guide eldercare.
- Understand the financial aspects of eldercare, including budgeting, insurance, and fraud prevention.

Action Plan

1. Identify Your Emotional Triggers

After reading about the emotional aspects, jot down situations that you find emotionally challenging. This will help you become more self-aware and better prepared.

2. Legal Checklist

Create a checklist of all the legal documents and considerations mentioned in the book. Consult with a legal advisor to ensure you're covering all bases.

3. Financial Audit

Conduct a financial audit based on the guidelines provided. This will give you a clearer picture of the financial resources available for eldercare.

4. Family Discussion

Schedule a family meeting to discuss the emotional, legal, and financial aspects of caring for your aging parent. Use this time to delegate responsibilities and make collective decisions.

5. Resource Compilation

Compile a list of resources, such as legal advisors, financial planners, and emotional support groups, that you can turn to for expert advice.

6. Reflect and Adjust

After implementing the initial steps, take time to reflect on what's working and what needs adjustment. Make the necessary changes and consult the book for additional guidance. By following this action plan, you'll be well-equipped to navigate the multifaceted challenges of eldercare with greater confidence and effectiveness.

Chapter 1 Introduction: A Global Perspective of Aging

Executive Summary

Welcome to the first chapter of our journey into understanding the landscape of eldercare. This chapter focuses on the aging population from a global perspective, a phenomenon that has far-reaching implications for families, healthcare systems, and economies. We'll delve into the key demographics and trends that are shaping this aging population, such as increased life expectancy, declining birth rates, and the impact of globalization. Understanding these macro-level shifts is crucial because they set the stage for the micro-level challenges that families face when caring for aging parents.

Key Points:

1. The global population is aging, with the number of people aged 60 and above expected to double by 2050.
2. Factors like increased life expectancy, declining birth rates, and globalization contribute to this demographic shift.
3. The aging population places a significant emotional, financial, and logistical burden on families.

Learning Objectives:

- Gain a comprehensive understanding of the global trends and demographics that are contributing to an aging population.
- Understand the economic and healthcare implications of an aging society.
- Recognize the impact of these demographic shifts on families, particularly in the role of caregiving for aging parents.

This chapter serves as the foundation for the rest of the book, providing you with the contextual knowledge you'll need to navigate the complexities of eldercare effectively.

Chapter 1:
A Global Perspective On Aging

The aging of the global population is a phenomenon that has been gradually unfolding over the past few decades. It's a shift that has profound implications, not just for economies and healthcare systems, but for families who find themselves in the role of caregivers for their aging loved ones. This chapter aims to provide a comprehensive overview of the demographics and trends shaping the aging population and the subsequent impact on families.

Demographics and Trends

The world is getting older, and the statistics are there to prove it. According to the United Nations, the number of people aged 60 years or older is expected to more than double by 2050. In developed countries, the demographic shift is even more pronounced, with the elderly population sometimes exceeding the younger population. Several factors contribute to this trend:

Increased Life Expectancy. Advances in healthcare and living conditions have significantly increased life expectancy. While this is undoubtedly a positive development, it also means that people are living long enough to develop age-related health issues that require care. The extended lifespan has implications for healthcare systems, retirement planning, and the overall structure of society. As people live longer, there's a growing need for long-term care, geriatric healthcare services, and adaptations in communities to be more age-friendly.

Declining Birth Rates. Many countries are experiencing declining birth rates, which means fewer young people to balance the demographic scale. This has implications for who will be available to provide care for the aging population. A smaller working-age population also means fewer people contributing to pension systems and public funds, which can lead to financial strain on social security systems. Additionally, the decline in birth rates could impact the economy, as a smaller workforce may contribute to reduced economic growth.

Globalization. In our increasingly interconnected world, younger generations often move away from their hometowns for education and job opportunities. This leaves a vacuum in the care structure for the elderly, who often remain in their communities. The migration of young people can lead to a lack of familial support for the elderly and can exacerbate feelings of isolation and loneliness among seniors. Furthermore, this trend necessitates alternative care structures, such as community care or professional caregiving services.

Economic Factors. The financial burden of caring for an aging population is immense. From pensions to healthcare, the economic systems in many countries are not adequately prepared for the silver tsunami. The increasing demand for elderly care services, coupled with the high costs of healthcare, can put significant pressure on both public and private finances. This may lead to increased taxes or reduced benefits for the elderly, which could further impact their quality of life.

Technological Advancements. Technology plays a crucial role in addressing the challenges posed by an aging population. Innovations in healthcare, such as telemedicine, wearable health devices, and AI-driven diagnostics, can help in managing the health of the elderly more effectively. Additionally, technology can aid in improving the quality of life for seniors through assistive devices, smart home technologies, and platforms that foster social connections. However, it's crucial to ensure that these technologies are accessible and user-friendly for the elderly population.

Policy Responses and Planning. Addressing the challenges of an aging population requires proactive policy responses and planning. Governments and organizations must develop strategies to support healthy aging, ensure adequate healthcare and social protection, and promote age-friendly environments. Policies must also focus on fostering intergenerational solidarity and leveraging the experience and skills of the elderly population. Preparing for an aging society is not just about addressing challenges but also about recognizing and harnessing the potential contributions of the elderly.

Conclusion

The aging of the global population is a multifaceted issue that requires a comprehensive approach, encompassing healthcare, economic planning, social support, technological innovation, and policy reform. It's an opportunity to reshape societies to be more inclusive, supportive, and respectful of the elderly, ultimately benefiting all generations.

Chapter 2 Introduction: Balancing Love and Responsibility

Executive Summary

Welcome to the second chapter of Part I, "Understanding the Landscape." In this chapter, we delve into the emotional aspects of eldercare, a dimension that is often overshadowed by logistical and financial concerns.

This chapter aims to guide you through the emotional labyrinth that caregiving often becomes. We'll focus on two key areas: the emotional challenges commonly encountered in eldercare and the importance of setting boundaries for your emotional well-being.

Key Points

- Understanding the emotional challenges in eldercare, such as guilt, stress, and role reversal.

- Learning the art of setting emotional boundaries to safeguard your well-being while providing effective care.

Learning Objectives

Comprehend the Emotional Landscape of Eldercare. Gain an understanding of the various emotional challenges that caregivers face in eldercare, including feelings of guilt, stress, and the complexities of role reversal when caring for an older family member.

Identify Emotional Challenges and Their Impact. Learn to identify common emotional challenges in eldercare and understand how they impact both the caregiver and the care recipient. This includes delving into the psychological and emotional strains that can arise in caregiving situations.

Develop Strategies for Emotional Management. Acquire skills for managing the emotional toll of caregiving. This includes techniques for coping with stress, managing feelings of guilt, and maintaining a healthy emotional balance.

Learn the Art of Setting Emotional Boundaries. Understand the importance of setting emotional boundaries to protect personal well-being. Learn practical strategies for establishing and maintaining these boundaries while still providing compassionate and effective care.

Balance Love and Responsibility. Explore ways to balance the dual roles of love and responsibility in the caregiving relationship. Understand how to maintain a compassionate approach to care while also addressing practical responsibilities and personal needs.

Navigate Role Reversal Dynamics. Gain insights into the dynamics of role reversal that often occur in eldercare, where children or younger family members become caregivers for their older relatives. Understand how to navigate these changes in family dynamics while maintaining respectful and loving relationships.

Promote Self-Care for Caregivers. Emphasize the importance of self-care for caregivers. Learn strategies for self-care that help maintain personal health and well-being, which is crucial for providing effective care to others.

Apply Emotional Intelligence in Caregiving. Develop an understanding of how emotional intelligence can be applied in the context of eldercare. Learn how to use empathy, self-awareness, and emotional regulation to improve caregiving interactions and outcomes.

By the end of this chapter, you should have a comprehensive understanding of the emotional dimensions of eldercare and be equipped with practical tools and strategies to manage these challenges effectively.

Chapter 2:
Balancing Love and Responsibility

Caring for an aging parent is an immense emotional, physical, and spiritual journey. It's an odyssey filled with complex feelings like love, guilt, frustration, and even resentment. This chapter aims to explore your journey of eldercare, focusing on the challenges you may face and offering strategies for setting emotional boundaries that can protect your well-being.

Emotional Challenges in Eldercare

Guilt. Sarah always felt she could do more for her aging mother, who had been diagnosed with Alzheimer's. One evening, she missed a call from her mother's care facility because she was at her son's school event. She later found out her mother had a fall. The guilt was overwhelming. Insight. Guilt can be paralyzing and can prevent you from making rational decisions about your parent's care.

Stress and Anxiety. For example, Mark juggled a full-time job and caring for his father, who had mobility issues. The constant worry about his father's well-being started affecting his performance at work. **Insight.** High levels of stress and anxiety can have a detrimental effect on your own health and well-being.

Role Reversal. Emily for example, once cared for by her mother, now found herself administering her mother's medications and helping her bathe. The shift was emotionally jarring. **Insight.**Transitioning from being cared for to being the caregiver can lead to feelings of inadequacy and strain the parent-child relationship.

Resentment. Here's an example. John felt resentment towards his siblings who lived out of state and didn't contribute to the daily caregiving tasks for their aging father. **Insight.** Resentment can arise when caregiving responsibilities are not equally shared among family members.

Isolation. Here's an illustration. Lisa, a single mother, spent her weekends caring for her aging mother. She started to miss social events and felt increasingly isolated. **Insight.** The time commitment required for caregiving can lead to social isolation.

Identity Crisis. Here's an illustration. After retiring, Karen devoted herself to caring for her husband with Parkinson's. Over time, she felt she was losing her own identity. **Insight.** Investing too much emotional energy in caregiving can overwhelm you.

Setting Boundaries for Emotional Well-being

Prioritize Self-Care. After months of neglecting her own needs, Sarah started setting aside Sunday afternoons for herself. This small change made her a more patient and effective caregiver. **Insight.** Taking time for yourself is essential for emotional relief.

Communicate Openly. Here's an example. Mark sat down with his siblings to discuss their father's care. They decided to hire a part-time caregiver, relieving Mark of some stress. **Insight.** Open communication is crucial for managing emotional challenges.

Seek Professional Help. Here's an example. Emily started seeing a therapist who helped her navigate the emotional complexities of her new caregiving role. **Insight.** Professional help can provide valuable coping strategies.

Set Emotional Boundaries. Here's an example. John set visiting hours for himself at his father's care facility, allowing him time to focus on his own family. **Insight.** Setting boundaries can help you manage your emotional well-being.

Delegate. Here's an example. Lisa enlisted her teenage children to help with some caregiving tasks, which allowed her to attend a friend's birthday party. **Insight.** Delegating tasks can lighten your load and allow you to maintain a social life.

Practicing Mindfulness. Here's an example. Karen took up meditation and found that it helped her manage her stress and maintain her sense of self. **Insight**. Mindfulness techniques can help you control your emotional responses.

Action Plan

1. **Self-Assessment.** Take some time to assess your emotional state. Acknowledge your feelings as the first step in managing them.

2. **Boundary Setting.** Use the guidelines provided to set emotional boundaries. Discuss these with other family members involved in caregiving.

3. **Seek Support.** Identify your support systems, such as family, friends, or professional counselors.

4. **Journaling.** Consider keeping an emotional journal for self-reflection.

5. **Review and Adjust.** Review your emotional boundaries and make adjustments as needed.

Conclusion

The emotional aspects of eldercare are often as challenging as the physical and logistical ones. By understanding the emotional challenges you may face and by setting appropriate boundaries, you can protect your emotional well-being without compromising the quality of care you provide. Balancing love and responsibility is not easy, but with the right emotional tools and boundaries, it is possible.

Chapter 3 Introduction:
Legal and Ethical Considerations

Executive Summary

Welcome to the third chapter of Part I, "Understanding the Landscape." As you navigate the complexities of eldercare, it's crucial to be aware of the legal and ethical considerations that come into play. This chapter, titled "Legal and Ethical Considerations," aims to provide you with a comprehensive understanding of the legal instruments and ethical dilemmas you may encounter.

From Power of Attorney to Living Wills and Advanced Directives, we'll explore the legal tools available to help you make informed decisions. Additionally, we'll delve into the ethical dilemmas that often arise in eldercare, such as end-of-life decisions and the distribution of caregiving responsibilities.

Key Points

1. Understanding the importance and implications of Power of Attorney.
2. Navigating the complexities of Living Wills and Advanced Directives.
3. Identifying and resolving ethical dilemmas in eldercare.

Learning Objectives

Gain a **comprehensive understanding of the legal tools** like Power of Attorney, Living Wills, and Advanced Directives, and how they can aid in eldercare.

Learn how to **navigate the ethical dilemmas** that often arise in eldercare, such as end-of-life decisions and caregiving responsibilities.

Acquire practical knowledge on how to initiate conversations about these sensitive topics with your aging parent and other family members.

This chapter serves as a **guide to help you navigate the legal and ethical maze of eldercare**, equipping you with the knowledge and tools you need to make informed decisions.

Chapter 3:
Legal and Ethical Considerations

Power of Attorney (POA)

Understanding the different types of Power of Attorney (POA) is crucial for effective eldercare planning. Each type serves a specific purpose and offers varying levels of control and responsibility to the appointed individual, known as the "attorney-in-fact" or "agent." Below, we delve into the **four main types of POA**, providing examples to illustrate their practical applications.

1. General Power of Attorney

A General Power of Attorney grants **broad powers** to the **attorney-in-fact**, allowing them to perform almost any act that the **principal**, or the person granting the power, could do themselves. This includes managing **financial** transactions, entering contracts, and making **healthcare decisions**.

How does this look? Sarah's father, Mr. Johnson, is going on an extended overseas trip. He signs a General POA appointing Sarah as his attorney-in-fact. With this document, Sarah can manage her father's bank accounts, pay his bills, and even sell or buy property on his behalf while he is away.

2. Limited or Special Power of Attorney

A Limited or Special Power of Attorney is much more restrictive than a General POA. It **specifies the particular actions** the agent is authorized to take on behalf of the principal.

It may look like this. Mark's mother needs surgery and will be incapacitated for a specific period. She signs a Limited POA that only allows Mark to manage her finances and medical decisions during her period of incapacitation.

3. Durable Power of Attorney

A Durable Power of Attorney remains in effect even if the principal becomes mentally incapacitated. **This type of POA is crucial for eldercare**, as it **ensures** that someone can **manage the affairs of an aging parent** if they **become unable** to do so themselves.

Here's an example. Emily's father has early-stage Alzheimer's. Knowing that his condition will likely worsen, he signs a Durable POA appointing Emily as his attorney-in-fact. This allows Emily to make financial and healthcare decisions for her father even if he loses the capacity to make those decisions himself.

4. Medical Power of Attorney

A Medical Power of Attorney, also known as a **Healthcare POA**, specifically grants the agent the **authority to make medical decisions** for the principal. This type of POA **activates** when the **principal is unable to make their own healthcare decisions.**

Here's how that may look. John's mother is diagnosed with a terminal illness. She signs a Medical POA appointing John as the person responsible for making healthcare decisions on her behalf. This allows John to consult with doctors and make critical medical decisions, such as approving or refusing treatments, if his mother becomes unable to do so.

How to Set Up a POA

First, consult with your family. It's crucial to discuss the decision of setting up a POA with family members or other significant individuals involved in the care and wellbeing of the person in question.

This discussion helps in ensuring that everyone understands the reasons for the POA, who will be appointed as the Attorney-in-Fact, and the scope of the authority being granted. It also helps in preventing conflicts or misunderstandings later on.

Second, choose an Attorney-in-Fact. The selection of a trustworthy and capable individual as the Attorney-in-Fact is one of the most critical steps. This person will have significant authority and responsibility, so it's important to choose someone who is reliable, understands the needs of the person they will be representing, and is willing to act in their best interests. It's often recommended to consider not just trustworthiness but also the geographical proximity, financial acumen, and the ability to handle potentially complex decisions.

Third, consult a lawyer. While there are do-it-yourself forms available, consulting a lawyer is strongly recommended to ensure that the POA meets all legal requirements and is tailored to the specific needs and circumstances of the individual. A lawyer can provide guidance on the types of POA available (such as durable, springing, financial, or medical), help articulate the scope of powers. **Fourth, sign and notarize.** Once the POA document is drafted, it must be signed and notarized to be legally binding. The person granting the power (the principal) must be mentally competent at the time of signing. The process of notarization varies by location but generally involves signing the document in front of a notary public. This step is essential to validate the identity of the principal and to confirm that the signature is genuine and made willingly.

Next, digitize and file the document, if necessary. Depending on the type of POA and local laws, it might be necessary to file the document with certain government offices, such as the local land records office if the POA includes authority to handle real estate transactions.

Then, communicate with financial institutions and other entities. Once the POA is established, it's important to inform financial institutions, healthcare providers, and other relevant entities about the POA. Providing them with a copy of the document may be required to authorize the Attorney-in-Fact to act on behalf of the principal.

And finally, review and update regularly. Circumstances can change, and it may be necessary to review and update the POA accordingly. Regular reviews ensure that the document remains relevant and reflects the current wishes of the principal. This is particularly important if there are changes in family dynamics, financial situation, or the health of the principal.

Living Wills and Advanced Directives

A Living Will is a written **statement detailing a person's desires** regarding **future medical treatment** in circumstances where they are **no longer able to express informed consent.** An **Advanced Directive is a broader** term that includes Living Wills and other documents like a Durable Power of Attorney for Health Care.

How to Set Them Up

1. **Discuss Wishes.** Have an open conversation with your aging parent about their medical preferences.

2. **Consult a Lawyer.** Legal advice can help tailor the document to your specific needs.

3. **Involve a Medical Professional.** healthcare provider can offer valuable insights into the medical implications of different choices.

4. **Sign and Store Safely**. Once the document is signed, store it in a safe but accessible place and provide copies to relevant parties.

Ethical Dilemmas in Eldercare

Ethical dilemmas in eldercare often revolve around issues like **end-of-life decisions**, **distribution of caregiving responsibilities** among **siblings**, and **balancing** the **autonomy** of the aging parent.

Three Types of Ethical Dilemmas

First, End-of-Life Decisions. How this may look. Jane's mother was in a coma with little chance of recovery. The family was divided on whether to continue life support, as her Living Will was ambiguous about this scenario. **Insight.** Issues like Do-Not-Resuscitate (DNR) orders and whether to continue aggressive treatment can be emotionally and ethically challenging.

Second, Distribution of Care. Here's an example. Mike and his two sisters had different views on who should be the primary caregiver for their aging father. Mike wanted to hire professional help, but his sisters insisted on family-based care. Insight. Deciding who among siblings or family members should bear the brunt of caregiving responsibilities can lead to ethical conflicts.

Third, Autonomy vs. Safety. Let's refer back to Emily. Emily's father, who had early-stage Alzheimer's, wanted to live alone. Emily had to weigh her father's desire for independence against the risks of him living alone. She ultimately decided that it was time for him to move into an assisted living community. Insight. Balancing the aging parent's desire for autonomy against the need for a safe environment can create ethical dilemmas.

How to Navigate Ethical Dilemmas

Open Dialogue. One of the key steps in navigating ethical dilemmas in eldercare is to maintain open lines of communication with all parties involved, including the elderly individual, family members, and caregivers. Open dialogue helps ensure that all perspectives are heard and understood. This includes discussing the values, preferences, and wishes of the elderly person, which are critical in making ethical decisions. It's also important to be open about potential conflicts, fears, and expectations to foster a transparent and honest environment.

Consult Professionals. In complex situations, consulting with ethicists, social workers, and lawyers can provide valuable perspectives. Ethicists, especially those specialized in medical or geriatric ethics, can offer guidance on moral considerations and ethical principles. Social workers are trained to handle sensitive family situations and can assist in navigating interpersonal dynamics. Lawyers, particularly those specializing in elder law, can provide legal perspectives, especially when decisions have legal implications. These professionals can help ensure that decisions are ethically sound and legally compliant.

Collective Decision-Making. Whenever possible, making decisions as a family or a group of involved parties ensures that everyone's views are considered. This approach fosters a sense of shared responsibility and can help in reaching a consensus that respects the wishes of the elderly individual while considering the well-being of all involved. In situations where family members have differing opinions, mediation or facilitated family meetings may be beneficial.

Respect Autonomy and Dignity. Always prioritize the autonomy and dignity of the elderly individual. Even in complex ethical dilemmas, their preferences, values, and rights should be at the forefront of any decision-making process. This may involve difficult conversations about end-of-life care, living arrangements, and medical treatment options.

Educate Yourself on Ethical Principles. Understanding basic ethical principles such as beneficence (doing good), non-maleficence (doing no harm), autonomy (respect for the individual's right to make decisions), and justice (fairness and distribution of resources) can be helpful. Educating yourself on these principles can provide a framework for evaluating and making ethical decisions.

Consider Long-Term Implications. Ethical dilemmas often have long-term implications. It's important to consider the future impact of decisions on the individual's quality of life, family dynamics, and legal or financial situations. Thinking ahead can help in making decisions that are sustainable and beneficial in the long run.

Document Decisions and Rationales. Keeping a record of decisions made and the rationales behind them is important, especially for future reference and in case of disputes. Documentation should include details of discussions, professional consultations, and the reasoning that led to the final decision.

Review and Adjust as Needed. Ethical dilemmas in eldercare are often evolving. Regularly reviewing and, if necessary, adjusting decisions as circumstances change is crucial. This ensures that decisions remain relevant and appropriate over time.

Navigating ethical dilemmas requires sensitivity, a thorough understanding of the issues at hand, and a commitment to the well-being and rights of the elderly individual. By following these steps, caregivers and families can approach these challenges thoughtfully and responsibly.

Action Plan

- **Legal Consultation.** If you haven't already, consult a lawyer to set up the necessary legal documents like POA and Advanced Directives.
- **Family Meeting.** Arrange a family meeting to discuss these legal and ethical considerations.
- **Medical Consultation.** Speak with healthcare providers to understand the medical implications of various choices in Advanced Directives.
- **Ongoing Review**. Periodically review all legal documents and ethical decisions to ensure they remain aligned with your loved one's wishes and needs.

Conclusion

The legal and ethical aspects of eldercare are complex but crucial. Understanding the importance of Power of Attorney, Living Wills, and Advanced Directives can save you and your family from future hardships. Being prepared for ethical dilemmas and knowing how to navigate them will help you provide care that aligns with your loved one's wishes and ethical considerations. This chapter serves as a guide to help you navigate these complicated but essential aspects of eldercare. Armed with this knowledge, you'll be better equipped to make informed, respectful, and loving decisions for your aging parent(s).

Chapter 4 Introduction:
Financial Planning for Eldercare

Executive Summary

Welcome to Chapter 4 of Part I, "Understanding the Landscape." As you embark on the journey of eldercare, one of the most critical aspects you'll encounter is financial planning. This chapter, titled "Financial Planning for Eldercare," aims to provide you with a comprehensive understanding of the financial elements involved in caring for an aging parent. We'll explore key areas such as Budgeting and Cost Analysis, Insurance and Government Assistance, and the ever-important topic of Financial Scams Targeting the Elderly.

Key Points

1. Understanding the importance of budgeting and conducting a thorough cost analysis for eldercare.
2. Navigating the complexities of insurance options and government assistance programs.
3. Recognizing and protecting against financial scams that specifically target the elderly.

Learning Objectives

• Gain a comprehensive understanding of how to budget for eldercare and conduct a cost analysis to prepare for both expected and unexpected expenses.

- Learn how to navigate the maze of insurance options and government assistance programs available for eldercare.
- Acquire the skills to identify and protect your aging parent from financial scams that prey on the elderly.

Financial planning for eldercare is a multifaceted endeavor that requires careful planning, keen awareness, and proactive measures. This chapter serves as a guide to helps equip you with the knowledge and tools you need to make informed financial decisions.

Chapter 4:
Financial Planning for Eldercare

Navigating the financial landscape of eldercare can be a daunting task. From budgeting for daily expenses to understanding the intricacies of insurance and government assistance, there's a lot to consider. This chapter aims to provide a comprehensive guide to financial planning for eldercare, focusing on Budgeting and Cost Analysis, Insurance and Government Assistance, and Financial Scams Targeting the Elderly.

Budgeting and Cost Analysis

Budgeting and cost analysis involve assessing your financial resources and estimating the potential costs of eldercare, such as medical expenses, in-home care, and assisted living facilities.

For example, Mary's father needed to move into an assisted living facility. She **assumed his pension** would **cover the cost, only to find out it was insufficient**. A thorough cost analysis could have helped her plan better.

Insight. A detailed budget and cost analysis will help you anticipate expenses, allowing you to make informed decisions and avoid or at least lessen financial strain.

Let's explore in more detail how to conduct a budget and cost analysis for an aging parent. This process is crucial for ensuring that their financial needs are met effectively

First, list all income sources. Start by compiling a comprehensive list of all income sources your aging parent has. This includes fixed incomes such as pensions, Social Security benefits, and any other regular income like annuities or investment returns. If your parent is still working or has rental properties, include these incomes as well. Also, consider potential income from selling assets or downsizing their home, if applicable. Ensure accuracy in this step, as it sets the foundation for the entire budgeting process.

Second, estimate expenses. Categorize and calculate all regular and potential expenses. This includes medical care costs, such as Medicare premiums, out-of-pocket expenses for medications, or any regular medical treatments. Housing costs are a significant part of expenses. Include rent or mortgage payments, property taxes, home insurance, and maintenance costs. Utilities should cover electricity, water, gas, phone, and internet services.

Other essential expenses may include groceries, transportation (including insurance and maintenance if they own a vehicle), and personal care items. It's also wise to consider the costs of any in-home care services or adult day care programs, if utilized.

Third, plan for contingencies. Setting aside funds for unforeseen expenses is crucial. This includes emergency medical care, which can be expensive and isn't always fully covered by insurance. Consider potential home repair costs, especially if living in an older home. It's also sensible to plan for increases in existing expenses, such as rising healthcare costs or inflation impacting daily living costs.

Review Periodically. Regularly revisiting the budget is essential as financial situations can change. This could be due to changes in income (like adjustments in Social Security benefits), or in expenses (like increased medical costs or changes in housing needs). A periodic review, perhaps annually or bi-annually, allows for adjustments to be made in time, ensuring that the budget remains realistic and effective.

This process also provides an opportunity to discuss finances with your aging parent, keeping them involved and informed about their financial health. This is not only beneficial for the immediate financial well-being of your aging parent but also for long-term planning, ensuring their comfort and security in their later years.

Understanding Medicare and Medicaid

In this section, I'll explore the various insurance options and government programs that can help offset the costs of eldercare. Let's delve deeper into Medicare and Medicaid, particularly focusing on their roles in the context of long-term care. Medicare, established in 1965, serves as a critical healthcare program for individuals 65 years or older, as well as for younger people with certain disabilities or End-Stage Renal Disease.

It's important to understand its four parts

1. Part A (Hospital Insurance)

This covers inpatient hospital stays, care in a skilled nursing facility, hospice care, and some home health care. For long-term care, Medicare Part A will cover a short stay in a skilled nursing facility, typically up to 100 days, if certain conditions are met, such as a prior hospital stay and the need for skilled nursing care.

2. Part B (Medical Insurance)

It covers certain doctors' services, outpatient care, medical supplies, and preventive services. However, it does not cover long-term care.

3. Part C (Medicare Advantage Plans)

These are Medicare-approved private plans that often include additional benefits and may have different rules for how you receive services.

4. Part D (Prescription Drug Coverage)

This part helps cover the cost of prescription drugs. It's crucial to note that Medicare does not cover custodial care if that is the only kind of care needed. Custodial care includes assistance with activities of daily living like bathing, dressing, and eating.

Medicaid Explanation

Medicaid, unlike Medicare, is not solely a federal program. It's a collaboration between states and the federal government, and thus, its rules and coverage can vary significantly from state to state. This program is **designed to assist low-income individuals** of **all ages** with their **medical expenses.**

Long-Term Care Coverage. Medicaid is the largest source of funding for medical and health-related services for low-income people in the U.S. This includes long-term care services, such as nursing home care and in some states, Medicaid also covers home and community-based services, allowing individuals to receive care in their own home or community rather than institutions.

Eligibility. To be eligible for Medicaid, applicants must meet federal and state requirements regarding income and assets. For instance, they might need to spend down their assets to qualify for Medicaid coverage for long-term care. The specifics can vary greatly based on individual circumstances and state regulations.

Medicaid Estate Recovery Program. It's also important to be aware of the Medicaid Estate Recovery Program, which seeks to recoup costs from the estates of deceased Medicaid recipients. Both Medicare and Medicaid play vital roles in the realm of eldercare, but their scopes and limitations are different. Understanding these programs thoroughly is essential for effective long-term care planning.

The Importance of Medicaid "Spend Downs."

This is where the concept of a Medicaid "Spend Down" comes into play. A "Spend Down" is essentially a legal way to "spend down" assets so that an individual can qualify for Medicaid. This often involves converting countable assets into exempt assets, such as purchasing an irrevocable funeral trust or making home improvements.

However, the rules governing "Spend Downs" are complex and vary by state. Making a mistake in the "Spend Down" process can result in a period of Medicaid ineligibility, leaving families with significant out-of-pocket costs. This is why consulting a lawyer who specializes in Medicaid "Spend Downs" is crucial. They can guide you through the intricacies of Medicaid eligibility, helping you make informed decisions that won't jeopardize your loved one's care or your family's financial stability.

Planning Decades in Advance

Given the complexities and limitations of both Medicare and Medicaid, it's evident that families must start planning for long-term care decades in advance. Relying solely on these government programs can lead to financial strain and limited care options.

Early planning allows families to explore other avenues like long-term care insurance, annuities, or even reverse mortgages as ways to finance long-term care. It also provides ample time to consult professionals, like Medicaid lawyers, to ensure that you're making the most out of available resources without risking future eligibility for essential programs.

The Veterans Administration Aid Attendance

The Veterans Administration (VA) Aid and Attendance program is a significant benefit for veterans and their surviving spouses who require assistance with daily living activities (ADLs). In this section, I aim to provide a comprehensive overview of the program, including eligibility criteria, benefits, and the application process.

What is the VA Aid and Attendance Program?

The Aid and Attendance program is particularly **beneficial for elderly veterans**. The benefit is a **monthly payment added to the amount of a monthly VA pension** for **qualified veterans** and **survivors**. It's designed to help those who need financial assistance for **in-home care** or to pay for an **assisted living facility**.

Eligibility Criteria

To be eligible for Aid and Attendance benefits, applicants must meet certain conditions. Please don't waste your time, the VA has to ration resources, so they weed out claimants who do not entirely meet their criteria:

First, the veteran has to have "qualifying military service." The veteran must have served at least 90 days of active military service, with at least one day during a wartime period. The veteran does not need to have served in combat.

Second, discharge status. The veteran must have been discharged under conditions other than dishonorable.

Third, age or disability. The program is available to veterans who are at least 65 years old or have a permanent and total disability.

Fourth, financial need. The VA looks at the veteran's income and net worth to determine financial need. The program is intended to assist those with a limited ability to pay for care.

Finally, daily living requirements. The veteran or spouse must require the aid of another person to perform personal functions required in everyday living or be bedridden, a patient in a nursing home, or have limited eyesight.

Benefits

The Aid and Attendance benefit provides a monthly payment on top of the regular VA pension. As of the last update*, the maximum benefit amounts were as follows:

- For a qualified veteran up to $1,936 per month
- For a qualified veteran and spouse up to $2,795 per month
- For a surviving spouse up to $1,244 per month

These amounts can change annually, so it's important to check the latest figures*.

Application Process

- Of course, it wouldn't be the government without bureaucracy. Fortunately, there are resources to help you with this process. You could consult a lawyer, although they're very expensive. You could contact your local Veterans Service Officer, although they're government employees with a heavy caseload.
- Or, you could contact an Accredited VA Claims Representative or Agent, who can help you prepare, present, and appeal your claim. The Accredited Claims Agent is your personal advocate who will focus on your claim. You can contact me for a free evaluation of your claim, see my contact information at the end of this book. So let's get started with the application process.
- Collect Necessary Documentation. This includes discharge papers (DD214 or equivalent), documentation of income, net worth information, proof of medical expenses, and a report from a physician detailing the need for Aid and Attendance.
- Fill Out the Right Forms. The main application form for Aid and Attendance is VA Form 21-2680 for veterans. For surviving spouses, the form is VA Form 21-0779.
- Submit the Application. Applications can be submitted to the pension management center that serves your state, or you can apply in person at a local VA office.
- Processing Time. The time it takes to process applications can vary. It's important to ensure that all necessary documentation is provided to avoid delays.

Social Security Disability Insurance

Expanding on the understanding of Social Security Disability Insurance (SSDI) requires delving into the nuances of this critical safety net, designed to provide support for those who find themselves unable to work due to a disability.

SSDI stands as a testament to the principle of collective care, offering financial assistance to individuals who have contributed to the Social Security system through their work history.

For Adult Children of Aging Parents (ACAPs), comprehending the intricacies of SSDI is paramount in advocating for and assisting their parents through potential eligibility and application processes.

SSDI is financed through payroll taxes collected under the Federal Insurance Contributions Act (FICA). **Eligibility for SSDI is based on the applicant having a sufficient "work credit" history**, meaning they have worked and contributed to the Social Security system for a certain number of years, with a portion of those years being recent. The number of work credits needed to qualify for SSDI depends on the age at which the person became disabled.

A Core Component of SSDI Is Its Strict Definition of Disability:

The Social Security Administration (SSA) defines a disability as a medical condition or combination of conditions that **significantly limit**s an individual's ability to **perform basic work activities**—and that is either expected to last for at least one year or result in death. This definition underscores the program's focus on long-term, rather than temporary, disabilities.

The **amount of the SSDI benefit is based on the applicant's earnings record**—the average amount of money they earned during their working years. This ensures that benefits are tailored to provide support in proportion to the contributions an individual has made to the Social Security system. Upon approval, beneficiaries may also become eligible for Medicare after a two-year waiting period, providing a crucial healthcare safety net.

For aging individuals, the onset of disability can be an unforeseen challenge, bringing not just physical and emotional distress but also financial uncertainty. SSDI offers a measure of security, acknowledging the dignity of every individual who has spent years contributing to the workforce. ACAPs play a crucial role in this process, helping to navigate the complexities of the SSDI application, ensuring their parents or aging loved ones receive the support they are entitled to.

The application process for SSDI can be daunting, requiring **detailed documentation of the applicant's medical condition**, work history, and ability to perform work-related activities. The SSA reviews applications with a critical eye, often necessitating appeals for initial denials. It's a process that demands patience, persistence, and a thorough understanding of the system's requirements.

Understanding SSDI is more than just knowing about a government program; it's about recognizing a vital resource available for our aging loved ones in their time of need. For ACAPs, this knowledge equips them to stand in the gap for their parents, ensuring that the transition into this phase of life is met with support, dignity.

The Sequential Analysis Process

Determining eligibility for SSDI involves a rigorous five-step process known as sequential analysis, employed by the Social Security Administration (SSA) to assess each claim:

1. **Work Status Evaluation**. The SSA first examines if the applicant is working and earning above a certain threshold. If not, the process moves to the next step.
2. **Severity of Condition**. The applicant's medical condition must significantly limit their ability to perform basic work activities for at least 12 months.
3. **Listed Medical Conditions**. The SSA checks if the condition is on its list of disabling conditions. If the condition is not listed, it must be of equivalent severity to qualify.
4. **Ability to Perform Past Work**. The analysis assesses whether the applicant can perform any of their past work despite the disability.
5. **Ability to Adjust to Other Work**. If unable to perform past work, the SSA considers age, education, work experience, and transferable skills to determine if the applicant can adjust to other work.

Each step of this analysis requires meticulous documentation and evidence, making the process both complex and time-consuming.

The Case for Professional Advocacy

Navigating the SSDI process can be overwhelming for ACAPs and their parents, where a single misstep can result in denial of benefits. This is where professional advocates become indispensable. Advocates, like myself, also know as **Authorized Representatives** specialize in SSDI claims. Here are offer several advantages of working with an advocate:

- **Expertise in SSDI**. Some advocates are medical professionals, for instance, I am an RN. Medical credentials enable advocates to have in-depth understanding of your medical condition(s). They possess deep knowledge of the SSDI process, including the intricate details of the sequential analysis, ensuring that applications are thoroughly and accurately completed.
- **Handling of Documentation**. They manage the extensive documentation required, from medical records to work history, reducing the burden on applicants and their families.
- **Representation**. In the event of an appeal, professional advocates can represent the applicant in hearings, significantly increasing the chances of a successful outcome.
- **No Upfront Costs**. Typically, SSDI advocates work on a contingency basis, meaning they only get paid if the claim is successful.

For ACAPs, the journey through SSDI claims can be fraught with challenges, but it's a path that need not be walked alone. Seeking the assistance of a professional advocate not only alleviates the stress and uncertainty of the process but also maximizes the chances of securing the benefits your parents rightfully deserve. In the intricate dance of caregiving, where every step counts, the support of a professional advocate in navigating SSDI claims can be the support that keeps the music playing, ensuring a future where financial support and care go hand in hand.

Action Plan

1. **Conduct a Budget and Cost Analysis**. Start by listing all income sources and estimating expenses. Plan for contingencies.

2. **Consult a Financial or Eldercare Advisor.** Get expert advice on insurance options and government assistance programs.

3. **Educate and Monitor.** Keep your aging parent informed about potential scams and regularly monitor their financial accounts for suspicious activities.

Conclusion

Financial planning for eldercare is a complex but crucial endeavor. Understanding the limitations of Medicare, especially its lack of coverage for long-term care, can save you from unexpected financial hardships. Exploring private insurance options like long-term care insurance can offer additional security. Being vigilant about potential financial scams can protect your aging parent from exploitation. This chapter serves as a comprehensive guide to help you navigate these complexities, equipping you with the knowledge and tools you need to make informed financial decisions in the realm of eldercare.

Chapter 5 Introduction:
End-of-Life Care and Planning

Executive Summary

The twilight years of our parents' lives bring forth a series of conversations and decisions that, although challenging, are saturated with love, respect, and the desire to honor their final wishes. "End-of-Life Care and Planning" is a chapter imbued with empathy and understanding, crafted to guide Adult Children of Aging Parents (ACAPs) through the intricacies of hospice and palliative care, funeral planning, and the preservation of legacy.

Through this exploration, we aim to equip you with the knowledge and sensitivity required to navigate these discussions, ensuring that the final chapter of your parents' journey is marked by dignity and a reflection of their life's story.

Key Points

1. **Demystifying Hospice and Palliative Care.** Understanding the distinctions and intersections between hospice and palliative care, and recognizing their pivotal role in providing comfort and dignity in life's final stages.

2. **The Importance of Advance Directives and Living Wills.** Emphasizing the critical role of advance directives and living wills in ensuring that end-of-life medical care aligns with your parents' wishes.

3. **Navigating Funeral Planning.** A compassionate guide to planning a funeral or memorial service that honors your parents' preferences and legacy.

4. **Legacy Preservation.** Encouraging conversations and projects that focus on preserving the memories, wisdom, and values your parents leave behind.

Learning Objectives

- **Identify and Understand End-of-Life Care Options.** Equip yourself with the knowledge to make informed decisions about hospice and palliative care, understanding when and how they can be integrated into your parents' care plan.
- **Prepare Advance Directives and Living Wills.** Learn how to initiate conversations about advance directives and living wills, ensuring your parents' health care preferences are documented and respected.
- **Plan Meaningful End-of-Life Ceremonies.** Gain insights into organizing funeral or memorial services that resonate with your parents' lives and values, including practical aspects of funeral planning.
- **Foster Legacy Conversations.** Encourage and participate in legacy preservation activities, ensuring that your parents' stories, values, and memories continue to inspire generations to come.

As we journey through this chapter, remember that the essence of end-of-life planning lies not in the logistics but in the love and respect we show for our parents' preferences and legacies. It's about creating a space where their final wishes are heard and honored, allowing them to conclude their life's story on their own terms.

Chapter 5:
End-of-Life Care and Planning

As we stand alongside our aging parents in the twilight of their lives, the conversations and decisions around end-of-life care become pivotal. This chapter is crafted with deep empathy and understanding, recognizing the emotional weight these topics hold for Adult Children of Aging Parents.

We delve into hospice and palliative care, funeral planning, and legacy conversations, aiming to guide you through these decisions with tenderness and respect, ensuring your parents' final wishes are honored with the dignity they deserve.

Understanding Hospice and Palliative Care

Hospice and palliative care are essential components of healthcare that focus on providing relief and comfort to individuals with serious illnesses, especially during the later stages of life. While they share some similarities in their approach to patient care, their focus, timing, and circumstances under which they are provided can differ significantly.

Hospice care is specifically designed for patients who are nearing the end of their life, typically when it is believed that the patient has six months or less to live, as determined by a physician.

The primary goal of hospice care is to provide comfort and maintain the highest quality of life possible for the remaining time. It is not about curing the illness but rather about caring for the individual in a holistic manner.

Key Aspects of Hospice Care:

1. The focus is on alleviating pain and other distressing symptoms such as nausea, breathing difficulties, and fatigue to ensure the patient is as comfortable as possible.

2. Hospice care includes counseling and support for the patient and their family to help them cope with emotional challenges and spiritual concerns.

3. Care is provided by a multidisciplinary team that includes doctors, nurses, social workers, therapists, counselors, and trained volunteers.

4. Hospice care can be provided in various settings including the patient's home, hospice centers, hospitals, or long-term care facilities.

Hospice care stands as a beacon of compassion and dignity at the end of life's journey, embodying a philosophy that prioritizes comfort, quality of life, and the holistic well-being of the individual. For Adult Children of Aging Parents (ACAPs), the decision to transition to hospice care is often fraught with emotion, signaling an acknowledgment of the finality of their parent's journey. Yet, within this decision lies a profound act of love and respect for their parent's wishes and well-being.

Hospice care provides a supportive environment where pain and symptoms are meticulously managed, allowing for moments of connection, closure, and peace in the final chapter of life. It's a choice that shifts the focus from the pursuit of curative treatments to the enrichment of the individual's remaining time with family and loved ones. This care is not just about easing physical discomfort but also about nurturing the emotional and spiritual needs of both the individual and their family, creating a space where every remaining moment is imbued with significance and love.

Understanding the essence of hospice care requires a recognition of its multidisciplinary approach, which includes medical professionals, counselors, social workers, and spiritual advisors, all working in concert to provide comprehensive care.

This team not only addresses the physical aspects of the patient's condition but also offers emotional support and guidance to families navigating this challenging time, ensuring that they, too, are cared for and supported.

The beauty of hospice care lies in its ability to bring solace and clarity in the midst of uncertainty, offering a pathway to celebrate life, honor legacy, and say meaningful goodbyes. For ACAPs, embracing hospice care for their aging parents means choosing a path of grace and dignity, ensuring that the final days are as comfortable and meaningful as possible, surrounded by the love and respect that their parents so richly deserve.

Let's see how it all might look. In the warmth of her beloved home, surrounded by the echoes of laughter and memories that had painted the walls of her life, an elderly woman faced the twilight of her existence with the dignity and courage that had defined her.

After a long battle with advanced-stage cancer, the time had come to shift the focus from seeking a cure to embracing comfort, ensuring her remaining days were filled with moments of love, serenity, and the gentle touch of care that hospice provides.

Choosing to receive hospice care at home allowed her to remain in the place most precious to her, enveloped by the familiarity and love that only home can offer.

As part of this tender transition, a dedicated hospice team became her companions on this final journey. A nurse, whose presence brought not only medical expertise but also a comforting aura, became a regular visitor, adeptly managing medications to ease discomfort and ensuring dignity in her most vulnerable moments.

This care allowed for clarity and the presence of mind to relish the time with her family, sharing stories, smiles, and the silent language of touch. A social worker, armed with a deep well of empathy, offered both the woman and her family the emotional support and guidance needed to navigate the complex tapestry of feelings and decisions that come with saying goodbye. Their expertise provided a beacon of light through the emotional fog, offering solace and understanding.

And there was the volunteer, whose visits brought not just practical help but also moments of joyous normalcy, a reminder of the beauty of everyday life amidst the shadows of farewell.

Their conversations, sometimes light and filled with laughter, sometimes deep and reflective, wove a comforting rhythm into her days, offering her family precious moments of respite and the peace of knowing she was not alone.

In her home, now a sanctuary of care, love, and dignity, the essence of hospice care unfolded beautifully. It was a journey not of solitude but of profound connection, ensuring her final chapter was not marked by the disease but by the grace of her spirit, the strength of her love, and the peace of being surrounded by her cherished ones.

This story, a testament to the compassionate embrace of hospice care, reflects the sacred passage to a dignified closure, surrounded by love, care, and the profound peace of coming home.

Palliative Care

Palliative care, on the other hand, can be provided at any stage of a serious illness and is not limited to the end-of-life scenario. It focuses on relieving symptoms, pain, and stress, regardless of the prognosis. Palliative care aims to improve the quality of life for both the patient and the family and can be provided alongside curative treatments.

Key Aspects of Palliative Care:
1. Similar to hospice, palliative care focuses on relieving symptoms like pain, shortness of breath, fatigue, constipation, nausea, loss of appetite, and difficulty sleeping.
2. It addresses a patient's physical, emotional, social, and spiritual needs.
3. Palliative care can be provided in conjunction with curative treatments and is not dependent on prognosis.
4. Involves a team of specialists including palliative care doctors, nurses, and other specialists who work together with a patient's other doctors to provide an extra layer of support.

Now let's look at an example. In the heart of his prime, Jose, a middle-aged man grapples with the unforgiving reality of congestive heart failure. Each day is a battle against the relentless tide of symptoms—shortness of breath that steals the ease of morning walks, fatigue that weighs down every step, transforming simple tasks into insurmountable challenges. It's a journey marked not just by the physical manifestations of his condition but by the shadow of anxiety and stress that clouds his spirit, a constant reminder of the fragility of life.

Enter the palliative care team, a beacon of hope and support in the midst of his storm. Collaborating closely with his cardiologist, they weave a tapestry of care tailored to his unique needs. Their expertise becomes the key to unlocking a better quality of life; they fine-tune his medications, not with the aim of a cure, which remains just beyond reach, but to bring relief and reclaim moments of joy that his heart condition has eclipsed. They offer nutritional guidance, transforming his diet into another tool against the swell of fluid retention, easing the burden on his weary heart.

But their care extends beyond the physical. They recognize the silent battle he wages against the anxiety and stress that accompany his illness, offering counseling that lights the dark corners of his worries, providing strategies to navigate his emotional turmoil. This holistic approach to care, emblematic of palliative medicine, underscores a fundamental truth: healing is not always about curing; sometimes, it's about living. Living with dignity, with moments of happiness snatched from the jaws of illness, with peace in place of pain.

Palliative care, in this story, is not a prelude to the end but a companion along the journey, enriching his life even as he continues to confront the realities of heart failure. It stands as a testament to the power of medicine that cares, supports, and comforts, ensuring that every patient's journey—whether it marches towards recovery or gently slopes towards a final rest—is navigated with compassion, dignity, and a profound respect for life at every stage. Consider a middle-aged man with congestive heart failure. He is undergoing treatment, but experiences severe shortness of breath and fatigue. A palliative care team works with his cardiologist to manage these symptoms. This includes adjusting medications to better control his heart failure symptoms, providing nutritional advice to manage his fluid retention, and counseling to help him cope with the anxiety and stress related to his illness. Palliative care in this scenario is not about end-of-life care but is focused on improving his quality of life as he continues with his heart failure treatments.

Both hospice and palliative care play vital roles in enhancing the quality of life for patients with serious illnesses. While hospice care is specifically for those at the end of life, palliative care can be beneficial at any stage of a serious illness. Both prioritize comfort, support, and the holistic well-being of the patient, ensuring that their journey, whether it is towards recovery or a peaceful end, is managed with dignity and compassion.

Planning for End-of-Life

Planning for end-of-life involves thoughtful considerations and preparations that can provide peace of mind for both the aging individual and their loved ones. This process includes setting up legal and healthcare documents and making decisions about the final stages of life. Advance directives are legal documents that outline a person's preferences for medical care if they're unable to make decisions themselves. This might include specifying whether they want life-sustaining treatments like resuscitation or artificial nutrition. Living wills specify more detailed wishes about end-of-life care, such as the desire for hospice care or avoidance of certain medical interventions.

Navigating the complexities of financial and legal planning for end-of-life care requires thoughtful preparation and open conversations to ensure that the final wishes of our aging loved ones are respected and fulfilled.

Estate planning, a cornerstone of this process, involves the meticulous organization of assets, financial affairs, and the distribution of property. It's a process that might see the establishment of trusts, the drafting of wills, and the designation of powers of attorney, ensuring that the legacy and hard-earned assets of our parents are managed according to their wishes.

Furthermore, making financial provisions for funeral expenses and discussing burial or cremation preferences are integral to honoring their final wishes with dignity.

Consider the scenario of an elderly man navigating the twilight of his life with a chronic heart condition. He takes proactive steps to outline his end-of-life care preferences through an advance directive, specifying no aggressive treatments like CPR. He meticulously plans the distribution of his assets among his children within his will and secures a funeral plan that encompasses all his preferred arrangements. This careful planning embodies a profound act of love and respect, ensuring his legacy is honored and his family is relieved of the burden of making these difficult decisions during a time of grief.

Initiating conversations about end-of-life wishes, while challenging, is essential for understanding and honoring the preferences of our loved ones. Choosing an appropriate time and place, approaching the topic with sensitivity, and listening with empathy are key to facilitating these discussions. It's about creating a space where fears and hopes can be shared openly, ensuring peace of mind for both our parents and ourselves.

Funeral planning further allows us to celebrate the life and honor the values of our loved ones. Whether through traditional services or personalized celebrations of life, these ceremonies are a reflection of the individual's personality and preferences. From choosing between burial and cremation to incorporating personal touches like favorite music or thematic elements, these plans are a final tribute to their unique journey through life.

Imagine a family gathering by a serene lakeside, the favorite fishing spot of their father, now passed. The air is filled with the soft melodies of his beloved jazz, and stories of his life and laughter are shared. This memorial, planned with his wishes in heart, becomes a beautiful, living memory of his spirit—a testament to a life well-lived and loved.

In these acts of planning and conversation, we weave the fabric of a legacy that transcends the material—ensuring that our parents' final chapter is written with the same love and dignity that marked their lives. It's a journey we take together, an act of profound respect that affirms the indelible mark they leave on our hearts and the world.

Preserving Legacy and Memories

In the journey of caregiving, the creation of a legacy project becomes a profound way to honor and preserve the essence of our loved ones. These projects not only serve as a therapeutic outlet during times of grief but also act as a bridge connecting generations, carrying forward the stories, wisdom, and experiences that define a life well-lived.

Imagine embarking on a project to capture the oral history or create a video biography of a beloved parent or grandparent. This could involve sitting down with them, a camera rolling gently in the background, as they weave the narrative of their lives through stories and reflections. It's an intimate process, one that captures the nuances of their voice, their laughter, and the depth of their experiences. Such recordings become invaluable, transforming into a timeless legacy that echoes their wisdom and love through the ages.

Similarly, crafting a memory book or scrapbook is akin to assembling a mosaic of a person's life. Each photograph, letter, and memento placed on its pages is a piece of the story they've lived, offering a tangible connection to the past. This book becomes a family treasure, a conduit through which future generations can glimpse the beauty and complexity of their ancestor's life.

The digital era offers another dimension of memory preservation through online sharing platforms. Setting up a dedicated website or digital album allows family and friends, near and far, to contribute to the tapestry of memories. It becomes a collective endeavor, a shared space where each contribution adds color and texture to the portrait of a life honored and remembered.

Consider the power of such a legacy project through the lens of one family's experience. They decide to create a video biography of their matriarch, capturing her recounting tales of yesteryears, her laughter filling the room as she narrates tales of past adventures, lessons learned, and the legacy she hopes to leave behind.

This video, rich with personal narrative and imbued with her essence, becomes a cherished artifact. It stands as a testament to her life, ensuring her stories, values, and love are carried forward, resonating with generations yet to come.

In crafting these legacy projects, we do more than preserve memories; we celebrate and honor the lives of those we hold dear, ensuring their stories continue to inspire, teach, and touch hearts long after they have gone. It is a gift of love, a tribute to their journey, and a beacon for those who will follow in their footsteps.

Action Plan

As Adult Children of Aging Parents (ACAPs), it's our heartfelt responsibility to ensure that our parents' final journey is navigated with love, respect, and in accordance with their wishes. This action plan is designed to guide you through the essential steps in managing end-of-life care and planning, aiming to provide clarity and support during this challenging time.

Here are six steps to compassionately and effectively manage end-of-life matters for our aging parents, ensuring their wishes are honored, and their dignity is upheld:

1. Understanding Hospice and Palliative Care Options

- Gather information on hospice and palliative care services. Understand the nuances and benefits of each to make informed decisions.
- Talk with your parents' doctors or care team to discuss their current health status and what care options are most suitable.
- Have a gentle conversation with your parents about these care options, listening to their preferences and concerns.

2. Setting Up Advance Directives and Living Wills

- Understand the importance and purpose of advance directives and living wills. This knowledge will help in making informed decisions.
- Consider consulting a lawyer who specializes in elder law to help draft these documents accurately.
- Involve family members in these discussions to ensure everyone understands and respects your parents' wishes.

3. Legal and Financial Planning

- Organize and review important documents like wills, insurance policies, and financial records.
- If not already done, assist your parents in estate planning, including the designation of powers of attorney.
- Understand the costs associated with end-of-life care and explore options like insurance, Medicare, or Medicaid.

4. Initiating Conversations About End-of-Life Wishes

- Find a calm and comfortable setting for these conversations.
- Approach the topic with sensitivity. Acknowledge that these conversations can be difficult, and provide reassurance and support.
- Keep a record of your parents' wishes as discussed, to refer back to when needed.

5. Planning for Funeral and Memorial Services

- Discuss with your parents their preferences for funeral or memorial services, including any specific traditions or personal touches they desire.
- Look into funeral homes, cremation services, or other arrangements as per their wishes. Plan for associated costs and logistics.
- Include siblings and other family members in planning, ensuring everyone has a role in honoring your parents' memory.

6. Preserving Memories and Legacy

- Engage in projects like making a family video, writing a memoir, or compiling a photo album that reflects your parents' lives and values.
- Spend time with your parents listening to their stories and life experiences, capturing these moments in audio or video if possible.
- Organize a way for friends and family to share memories, perhaps through a digital platform or a memory book.

Conclusion

Navigating the end-of-life journey with our parents is a sacred and tender path. This chapter is designed to walk you through these delicate conversations and decisions with warmth, understanding, and practical guidance. By carefully considering hospice and palliative care options, thoughtfully planning for the end of life, and celebrating their legacy, we can ensure that our parents' final chapter is handled with the love, respect, and dignity they deserve.

Overview of Part II

Executive Summary

Part II, "Managing Eldercare Remotely," is designed to equip you with the tools and strategies needed to provide effective care for your aging parents from a distance. The focus is on leveraging technology, building a reliable care team, and ensuring seamless communication to make remote eldercare a viable option.

Key Points:

1. Assessment and Planning

The first step in remote eldercare is understanding the specific needs of your aging
parent. This chapter guides you through conducting a comprehensive needs assessment and creating a tailored care plan.

2. Technology to the Rescue

Technology can be a game-changer in remote eldercare. This chapter explores various technological solutions like telehealth services and remote monitoring systems that can make your life easier.

3. Building Your Care Team

No one can manage eldercare alone. This chapter helps you identify and coordinate
with local resources and caregivers to ensure your parent receives the best care possible.

4. Communication Strategies

Effective communication is crucial when managing care from a distance. This chapter offers strategies for maintaining open lines of communication with both your aging parent and your care team.

Learning Objectives:

● Learn how to conduct a needs assessment and develop a personalized care plan for your aging parent.

● Understand the role of technology in facilitating remote eldercare and become proficient in using relevant platforms.

- Acquire skills to build, manage, and communicate effectively with a remote care team.
- Develop crisis management strategies for handling emergencies remotely.

Chapter 6 Introduction: Assessment and Planning

Welcome to Chapter 6, the first chapter of Part II, "Managing Eldercare Remotely." As the landscape of eldercare evolves, so does the need for eldercare strategies. In this chapter, titled "Assessment and Planning,," my aim is to equip you with the essential tools and knowledge to manage your aging parent's care from a distance effectively. We will delve into two critical components: Conducting a Needs Assessment and Creating a Care Plan.

Key Points:

- The importance of a **comprehensive needs assessment** to understand the specific requirements of your aging parent.
- The steps involved in creating a robust care plan that addresses both **immediate** and long-term needs.

Learning Objectives:

1. Understand how to conduct a thorough needs assessment, including evaluating medical conditions, daily living activities, and emotional well-being.
2. Learn how to create a comprehensive care plan that outlines the types of care required, identifies potential caregivers, and establishes a schedule and budget
This chapter serves as a guide to help you navigate these critical initial steps, providing you with the framework to make informed and effective decisions for your aging parent's care, even from afar.

Chapter 6:
Assessment and Planning

The advent of technology and the changing dynamics of family structures have made remote eldercare a viable, albeit challenging, option. This chapter focuses on two pivotal aspects of managing eldercare from a distance: Conducting a Needs Assessment and Creating a Care Plan.

Conducting a Needs Assessment

Your needs assessment is a comprehensive evaluation of your aging parent's physical, emotional, and social requirements. It serves as the foundation for a care plan. Imagine you're building a house. You wouldn't start without a blueprint, would you?

Similarly, a needs assessment is the blueprint for your parent's care plan. Without it, you're essentially building a house without a foundation. **Insight.** A thorough needs assessment can help you identify the specific types of care your parent needs, thereby allowing you to allocate resources more effectively.

How to Conduct a Needs Assessment

First, the medical evaluation. Consult healthcare providers for a complete medical assessment, including any chronic conditions, medications, and potential future health issues. I highly recommend using the online patient portal that most healthcare systems offer these days. Second, assess you parent's activity of daily living (ADLs). Assess the ability of your parent to perform daily activities like bathing, eating, and mobility.

If they need help with two of their ADLs this will help establish the "medical necessity" for many in-home care services. Third, emotional and social needs. Evaluate the emotional well-being of your parent, including any signs of depression or loneliness. Finally, the financial assessment. Understand the financial resources available for care, including insurance, pensions, and savings.

Your Care Plan

A care plan is a detailed roadmap outlining the types of care your parent requires, the potential caregivers, and a schedule and budget for the care. Think of a care plan as a GPS for eldercare. Just as you wouldn't embark on a road trip without a GPS, you shouldn't start eldercare without a care plan. **Insight.** A well-crafted care plan ensures that all needs identified in the assessment are met, reducing the risk of neglect or inadequate care.

How to Create a Care Plan

Creating a care plan is a critical step in ensuring that your aging loved one receives the appropriate care they need. Let's delve into each component of a care plan with specific examples to provide a clearer understanding of how to go about this crucial task.

First, Let's Look at the Types of Care. **Medical Care.** Let's say your mother has been diagnosed with Alzheimer's disease. Based on the needs assessment, you know she will require specialized medical care, including regular check-ups, medication management, and possibly even specialized Alzheimer's care services.

Second, Let's look At **Custodial Care.** For example, your father has mobility issues and struggles with daily activities like bathing and dressing. This is custodial care, which focuses on assisting with daily living activities, becomes a necessity for your father's quality of life. However, **Medicare** and most private medical insurance **absolutely does no**t pay for **"custodial care!"**

Third, Let's Look at **Emotional Support.** For example, your parents live alone and have been showing signs of loneliness and depression. Emotional support, perhaps in the form of regular companionship or counseling, should be included in the care plan. You really have to be proactive in this area because many of your parents' friends will probably have passed away.

Select Caregivers

First, Let's Consider **Professional Caregiver for Medical Needs.** For instance, for your mother's Alzheimer's care, you might opt for a professional caregiver trained in dementia care. One example is **Certified Dementia Practitioner**® (CDP). Another example is the Certified Senior Advisor (CSA), which I have held for several years. Of course, there aren't any guarantees of a caregiver's work ethic, compassion, or competence, but this helps ensures that she receives specialized attention.

Second, Let's Look at **Family Members for Custodial Care.** It's say to say, many families aren't all of the same page—honestly, many families are outright dysfunctional and hostile. However, I hope that your siblings who live close to your father and can take turns assisting him with daily activities. Obviously, this arrangement can provide the custodial care he needs without the added cost of hiring a professional.

Third, **Combination of Caregivers** for Emotional Support. You can schedule regular video calls for companionship and hire a local counselor for in-person emotional support, thereby using a combination of family and professionals for this aspect of care.

Create a Schedule

First, **Medical Care Schedule**. Let's say, that your mother's **Alzheimer's** medication needs to be administered twice a day. A professional caregiver can visit in the morning and late afternoon for this purpose. An unlicensed home health aide can also so this by simply assisting with pre-organized medicine. Second, **Custodial Care Schedule**. Your siblings can create a rotating schedule where each takes a day of the week to assist your father with his daily activities. Third, **Emotional Support Schedule**. You can set up weekly video calls with your parents every Sunday, and the local counselor can visit them every Wednesday.

Budget and Financial Planning

First, Budgeting for Professional Care. This is main problem that most families face, they didn't anticipate having to pay out of pocket for in-home care. Most families **mistakenly assume** that Medicare will pay for "custodial care." The stark fact is that specialized Alzheimer's care for your mother could cost around $25 per hour. If the caregiver visits for two hours a day, that's $50 a day or $1,500 a month. You'll need to allocate this amount in your budget. This is a gross understatement, you should probably start saving decades in advance for such a major expense. One example would be a Long-term Care Insurance policy.

Second, Budgeting for Family-provided Care. While family-provided care may not have a direct cost, there could be indirect costs like gas for travel. These should be accounted for in the budget. Third, Budgeting for Emotional Support. The weekly counseling sessions for your parents might cost around $100 per session, adding up to $400 a month. This, along with any costs for video calling software or equipment, should be included in the budget.

Creating a care plan is not a one-size-fits-all process; it requires thoughtful consideration of the unique needs of your aging loved one. By identifying the types of care needed, selecting appropriate caregivers, establishing a schedule, and budgeting accordingly, you can create a comprehensive care plan that serves as a roadmap for your family. This ensures that your loved one receives the best care possible, tailored to their specific needs, even when you're managing it from a distance.

Action Plan

1. **Conduct a Needs Assessment**. Start by consulting healthcare providers, evaluating daily living activities, assessing emotional needs, and understanding financial resources.

2. **Create a Care Plan**. Based on the needs assessment, identify the types of care required, select caregivers, establish a schedule, and allocate financial resources.

3. **Review and Update**. Periodically review and update the care plan to accommodate any changes in your parent's condition or needs.

Managing eldercare remotely is a complex task that requires meticulous planning and execution. The first step is conducting a comprehensive needs assessment to understand the specific requirements of your aging parent. This assessment should cover medical conditions, daily living activities, emotional well-being, and financial resources.

Once you have a clear picture of the needs, the next step is to create a care plan. This plan should outline the types of care required, identify potential caregivers, and establish a schedule and budget for the care.

I can't emphasize the importance of these steps enough! Your well-conducted needs assessment ensures that you have a clear understanding of your parent's requirements, allowing you to allocate resources effectively.

A well-crafted care plan serves as a roadmap for providing this care, reducing the risk of neglect or inadequate care. Together, these tools provide you with the framework to make informed and effective decisions for your aging parent's care, even from a distance.

Conclusion

While remote eldercare presents unique challenges, a thorough assessment and planning process can significantly ease these difficulties. This chapter serves as a comprehensive guide to help you navigate these critical initial steps, equipping you with the framework to make informed and effective decisions for your aging parent's.

Chapter 7 Introduction: Eldercare Technology

Welcome to Chapter 7. In today's digital age, technology has become an invaluable asset in virtually every aspect of our lives, and eldercare is no exception. This chapter, aptly titled "Technology to the Rescue," I aim to guide you through the technological solutions available for managing eldercare from afar.

Key Points

- The role of Telehealth and Remote Monitoring in providing medical care and supervision.
- The utility of various Apps and Platforms designed specifically for care coordination among family members, caregivers, and healthcare providers.

Learning Objectives

1. Understand how **telehealth** can be used to consult with healthcare providers, manage medications, and monitor chronic conditions.

2. Gain insights into remote monitoring technologies that can track vital signs, activities, and even detect falls.

3. Become familiar with apps and platforms that facilitate care coordination, from scheduling to medication reminders, and how to choose the one that best fits your needs.

Eldercare is rapidly evolving, and technology is playing an increasingly significant role in shaping it. Whether it's telehealth consultations that eliminate the need for physical doctor visits or apps that help you coordinate care among family members, technology offers innovative solutions to the challenges of remote eldercare.

This chapter will equip you with the knowledge to leverage these technologies effectively, ensuring that your aging loved ones receive the best care possible, even when you can't be there in person.

Chapter 7:
Technology to the Rescue

The digital revolution has permeated every aspect of our lives, and eldercare is no exception. As the world becomes increasingly interconnected, technology offers innovative solutions to the challenges of remote eldercare. This chapter focuses on two key technological advancements that are reshaping the way we manage eldercare from a distance: Telehealth and Remote Monitoring, and Apps and Platforms for Care Coordination.

Telehealth in Geriatrics

Telehealth is not merely a technological advancement; it's a paradigm shift in healthcare delivery. This shift is particularly impactful in the realm of geriatric care, where the challenges of mobility, chronic illness, the threat of COVID, flu, and RSV, and specialized needs are ever-present. Let's delve deeper into how telehealth can be a game-changer for older adults.

Chronic Disease Management

Diabetes and Hypertension. Older adults often grapple with multiple chronic conditions. Telehealth platforms can integrate data from glucose monitors and blood pressure cuffs, allowing healthcare providers to make real-time adjustments to treatment plans. This is crucial for preventing complications like diabetic neuropathy or hypertensive emergencies.

Heart Conditions. With the aid of wearable technology, cardiologists can remotely monitor heart rhythms and other cardiovascular indicators. This is invaluable for timely interventions, especially in conditions like atrial fibrillation that may require rapid medication adjustments.

Cognitive Health

Dementia and Alzheimer's disease. Telehealth can be instrumental in the early diagnosis and ongoing management of cognitive decline. Virtual cognitive assessments can be administered, and medication effectiveness can be monitored without the stress of a clinic visit, which can exacerbate symptoms for dementia patients.

Mental Health

Depression and Anxiety. Mental health issues are often underdiagnosed in the elderly. Telepsychiatry can provide a less intimidating avenue for older adults to seek help. Regular virtual sessions can help in both diagnosing and treating emotional disorders, which are often exacerbated by isolation.

Mobility and Physical Therapy

Arthritis and Musculoskeletal Issues. Physical therapists can guide patients through exercises via video consultations, ensuring correct form and technique. This is particularly beneficial for those with mobility issues who find it challenging to attend in-person sessions.

Medication Management

Polypharmacy. Older adults are often on multiple medications, increasing the risk of adverse interactions. Telehealth allows for a comprehensive review of all medications, ensuring they are necessary, effective, and safe when taken in combination.

If you're an adult child concerned about your aging parent's health, the issue of medication management should be high on your radar. The term "polypharmacy" might sound like medical jargon, but it's something you'll want to understand. It refers to the use of multiple medications at the same time, and it's particularly common among older adults.

While medications are often necessary, juggling several of them can lead to harmful interactions, known as adverse drug reactions (ADRs). Also, don't forget about vaccinations and screening. Virtual consultations can help in planning and scheduling necessary vaccinations and screenings like mammograms or colonoscopies. This ensures that preventive measures are not overlooked.

What the Research Tells Us

Veterans Study. A study focused on older veterans found that unplanned hospital visits often occurred due to harmful interactions between medications. This is a wake-up call for families to keep an eye on the medications their elderly loved ones are taking.

Hospital Admissions. Another study showed that almost half of the adults admitted to medical wards had drug-related problems, including harmful medication interactions. If your parent has multiple health issues and is on various medications, this is something to be vigilant about.

Cancer Patients. In a study of patients with cancer, over 21% of hospital admissions were due to adverse drug reactions. While this study was not exclusively on older adults, the implications are clear: managing medications is crucial, especially if your parent is dealing with a serious illness like cancer.

Financial Cost. Lastly, a study in England found that these adverse drug reactions are not only harmful but also costly. The study estimated that the annual cost to the healthcare system could be in the billions. This underscores the societal impact of this issue.

What This Means for You and Your Aging Parent

Be Proactive. Don't wait for a health crisis to review your parent's medications. Make it a routine part of their healthcare. Consult the Experts. Involve healthcare providers in medication management. They can help identify potentially harmful drug interactions. Stay Informed. The more you know, the better you can advocate for your parent's health.

Research, ask questions, and consult with healthcare providers. Look at the Big Picture. This isn't just about avoiding bad drug interactions; it's about enhancing your parent's overall quality of life. Proper medication management can lead to better health outcomes and more independence for your parent. So, if you're helping to manage your aging parent's health, take the issue of polypharmacy seriously. It's not just a matter for doctors and pharmacists; it's a family affair.

The Role of Telehealth in End-of-Life Care

If you're an adult child navigating the emotional and complex journey of end-of-life care for an aging parent, the role of telehealth can be a game-changer. It's not just about convenience; it's about providing a compassionate, personalized, and dignified experience for your loved one during their final chapter. Let's delve into how telehealth can be a supportive partner in this journey.

Discussions and Planning

One of the most challenging aspects of end-of-life care is initiating those difficult conversations about treatment preferences, Do-Not-Resuscitate (DNR) orders, and estate planning. Telehealth can facilitate these discussions in a more comfortable setting—your parent's home. It allows for multi-party video calls, enabling family members who may be geographically dispersed to participate in these conversations.

Symptom Management

As your parent's health declines, symptom management becomes increasingly important. Pain, breathlessness, or nausea can be debilitating. Telehealth allows for real-time consultations with healthcare providers to adjust medications or other treatments. This immediacy can be a significant relief for your parent and reduce the stress of emergency hospital visits.

Emotional and Spiritual Support

End-of-life care isn't just about managing physical symptoms; it's also about emotional and spiritual well-being. Telehealth can connect your parent to counselors, spiritual advisors, or even support groups who specialize in end-of-life care. These virtual sessions can offer a sense of peace and closure, both for your parent and the entire family.

Hospice Care

When curative treatments are no longer effective or desired, hospice care becomes an option. Telehealth can complement traditional hospice services by providing additional layers of support. Virtual check-ins can supplement in-person visits, ensuring that your parent's comfort and dignity are maintained.

Family Support

As an adult child, you're not just a caregiver; you're also coping with your own emotional journey. Telehealth can offer you access to support groups and counselors specializing in grief and bereavement. These services can help you navigate the emotional complexities of this life stage, offering coping strategies and a supportive community.

What This Means for You and Your Family

First, Personalized Care. Telehealth allows for a more tailored approach, respecting your parent's wishes and unique medical needs. Second, Convenience and Comfort. The ability to receive consultations and support from the comfort of home can be a significant relief for both you and your parent.

Third, Family Involvement. Telehealth enables the whole family to be involved in the care process, regardless of where they are located. Fourth, Holistic Support. Beyond medical care, telehealth offers avenues for emotional and spiritual support, enriching the quality of your parent's final days. Finally, Empowerment. Knowledge is power. Telehealth can provide you with the resources and support you need to make informed decisions about your parent's care.

End-of-life care is a deeply personal and emotional journey, not just for your aging parent but for you and your family as well. Telehealth can be a valuable ally in this journey, offering a blend of medical, emotional, and logistical support that can make this challenging time a bit more manageable. It's not just about extending life; it's about enhancing the quality of life for everyone involved.

Chapter 8 Introduction: Building Your Care Team

Executive Summary

Welcome to Chapter 8, and Part II, "Managing Eldercare Remotely." As you navigate the complexities of remote eldercare, one of the most crucial steps is assembling a reliable care team. In this chapter, titled "Building Your Care Team," I'll guide you through the process of identifying local resources and hiring and managing caregivers effectively.

Key Points

- The importance of identifying local resources, such as healthcare providers, community centers, and emergency services, that can assist in your parent's care.
- A comprehensive guide to hiring and managing caregivers, including background checks, and contracts.

Learning Objectives

1. Understand how to **identify** and **leverage local resources** that can assist in your parent's care.

2. Gain insights into effectively managing caregivers to ensure the highest quality of care for your aging parent.

Chapter 8:
Building Your Care Team in Remote Eldercare

If you're reading this, chances are you're an adult child grappling with the complexities of managing your aging parent's care from a distance. You're not alone. As our parents age, the roles often reverse, and we find ourselves becoming their caregivers. But what happens when you can't be there in person? That's where building a strong care team comes into play. In this chapter I'll guide you through the process of identifying local resources and hiring and managing caregivers, all while you're miles away.

Identifying Local Resources

Before you even think about hiring a caregiver, it's crucial to know what local resources are available to your parent. These can range from healthcare providers to community centers offering senior activities, to emergency services.

Let's Look Into Selecting Healthcare Providers

Primary Care Physicians. Make sure your parent has a local doctor who understands their medical history and can provide regular check-ups. Your primary should also be actively coordinating your care among your specialists like cardiologists, neurologists, or orthopedic doctors.

I also recommend seeking a practitioner who is experienced in caring for elderly patients—you may even want to pick a geriatrician (i.e., a doctor who specializes in treating elderly patients). This is good place to mention nurse practitioners (NPs).

A Geriatric Nurse Practitioner is a specialized nurse who holds an advanced degree in nursing, typically a Master's or Doctorate, and has received specialized training and certification in the care of older adults. Geriatric Nurse Practitioners focus on the comprehensive health needs of the elderly, addressing not just physical health but also the psychological and social aspects of aging. In other words, the NP does many the same things as a doctor—but usually with more compassion. Don't get bogged down with the world-wind of abbreviations, the main one is Advanced Practice Registered Nurse (APRN).

Their role encompasses a wide range of responsibilities, including:

First, **Assessment.** NPs conduct thorough health assessments, considering the unique health challenges faced by older adults, such as chronic conditions, mobility issues, and cognitive impairments.

Second, **Diagnosis and Treatment.** They are qualified to diagnose and manage a variety of health conditions, prescribe medications, and develop treatment plans.

Third, **Preventive Care.** They focus on preventive care measures to maintain the health and well-being of elderly patients, including vaccinations, screening tests, and lifestyle counseling.

Fourth, **Education and Counseling.** NPs provide education to patients and their families about managing health conditions, medication management, nutrition, and other aspects of elderly care.

Finally, **Coordination of Care.** They often coordinate care among various healthcare providers and services, ensuring a holistic approach to the patient's health.

Geriatric Nurse Practitioners are often more accessible than physicians in a medical office for several reasons:

First, **Availability.** NPs may have more flexibility in their schedules, allowing for quicker appointment scheduling and often providing longer consultation times compared to physicians. Second, **Distribution.** They are sometimes more readily available in various settings such as community clinics, long-term care facilities, and home health settings, making them more accessible to patients who may have mobility or transportation issues.

Third, **Holistic Approach.** Their training in both the medical and psychosocial aspects of aging allows NPs to offer a comprehensive approach to care that can be particularly beneficial in managing the complex health needs of older adults. In other words, they usually have better bed-side manners.

Fourth, **Continuity of Care.** NPs often provide continuity of care, building long-term relationships with patients and families, which can be particularly important in managing chronic conditions common in older age.

Next, Let's Look At Community Centers and Services

First, **Senior Centers**. Caregivers often overlook their local senior center. They offer a range of activities and services, from exercise classes to meal programs, that can enrich your parent's life. Second, **Transport Services**. Some communities offer transportation services specifically for seniors, which can be a lifeline for those who no longer drive.

Second, **Local Hospital**. Know the closest hospital to your parent's home and the services they offer. Third, **Emergency Contacts**. Have a list of neighbors or local friends who can check on your parent in case of an emergency. Last but certainly not least, **Local Area Agency on Aging**. For **Adult Children of Aging Parents (ACAPs)**, the local **Area Agency on Aging (AAA)** can be an **invaluable resource** in developing and implementing effective caregiving strategies.

These agencies, available nationwide, are designed to support older adults, caregivers, and families in various aspects of aging and caregiving. Here's how AAA can fit into and enhance your caregiving strategies:

Information and Referral Services

First, **Understanding Options**. AAAs provide information on a wide range of services available for older adults, including in-home care, meal programs, transportation services, and more. This can help you make informed decisions about the types of support your aging parent might need.

Second, **Resource Navigation**. They can assist in navigating the often complex world of eldercare services, helping you find the most appropriate resources in your area.

Caregiver Support Programs

First, **Education and Training**. AAAs often offer workshops and training programs for caregivers, which can equip you with the necessary skills and knowledge to provide effective care for your aging parent. Second, **Support Groups**. Many AAAs facilitate support groups where you can connect with other caregivers, share experiences, and learn from each other. They also provide care planning assistance.

Assessment and Care Planning

First, **Needs Assessment**. AAAs can conduct assessments to determine the specific needs of your aging parent, which is crucial in creating a tailored care plan. Second, **Care Coordination**. They can help coordinate various services and supports to ensure that your parent's needs are met comprehensively. In some cases they can actually help you directly.

Direct Assistance

First, **In-Home Services**. Some AAAs provide or can connect you with in-home services like personal care, housekeeping, and meal delivery, which can be crucial in allowing your parent to age in place safely. I personally have benefited from this invaluable and time saving task of assembling and vetting a list of credible care providers for my parents. Second, **Respite Care**. They can also assist in arranging respite care, giving you a much-needed break and preventing caregiver burnout. I can't emphasize this enough...**Respite care for your weary caregivers is critical!** The AAA can also help with advocacy and legal aid, financial assistance programs, and accessibility and modification services.

Advocacy and Legal Aid

Advocacy Services. AAAs can offer guidance on legal matters related to aging, including healthcare directives, power of attorney, and elder rights. **Medicare and Insurance Counseling.** They often provide counseling services to help you and your aging parent navigate Medicare and other insurance-related issues.

Financial Assistance and Modification Programs

Financial Guidance. AAAs can provide information on financial assistance programs for which your parent may be eligible, including help with medical costs, energy bills, and more. **Home Safety Assessments.** They can assist in assessing the home for safety and recommend modifications to enhance livability and accessibility.

Incorporating the services of your local Area Agency on Aging into your caregiving strategy can significantly ease the burden of managing care. They not only provide direct services and resources but also offer guidance, support, and a connection to a broader community of care – all of which are essential in ensuring the best possible quality of life for your aging parent.

Hiring and Managing Caregivers

While local resources are invaluable, most aging parents will also need some level of personal care, whether it's help with daily activities, medication management, or companionship.

The Hiring Process

First, **Needs Assessment**. Before you start the hiring process, conduct a thorough needs assessment to determine the level and type of care your parent requires. Second, **Interviews**. Conduct interviews with potential caregivers. Make sure to ask about their experience, qualifications, and references. I might add, that there's a fine line between being all-star advocate and alienating your potential allies*. In other words, most of the time it's better to use finesse than to be a "helicopter mom."

Make no mistake about, there is a labor shortage of home health aides. It's very difficult for home care agencies to recruit and retain competent compassionate staff. Third, **Background Checks**. Never skip this step. A background check can provide crucial information about a caregiver's history. Fourth, **Contracts**. Draft a contract outlining the caregiver's responsibilities, hours, and compensation. This protects both parties and sets clear expectations.

Managing Caregivers

First, **Orientation**. Once you've hired a caregiver, provide them with a thorough orientation. This should include a tour of your parent's home, an introduction to any home healthcare devices, and a discussion of your parent's daily routine and preferences. Second, **Regular Check-ins**. Schedule regular check-ins with the caregiver to discuss your parent's condition, any concerns, and possible adjustments to the care plan. Third, **Conflict Resolution**. If conflicts arise, address them immediately.

Action Plan

1. **Research Local Resources**. Start by identifying local healthcare providers, community services, and emergency contacts that can assist in your parent's care.

2. **Hiring Process**. Understand the legal and practical aspects of hiring a caregiver, including background checks and contract agreements.

3. **Management and Oversight**. Learn how to manage caregivers effectively, including setting expectations, regular check-ins, and conflict resolution.

Chapter 9 Introduction: Delegating to Friends, Family, Church, and Community Groups

Executive Summary

In the intricate journey of eldercare, the weight of responsibility often rests heavily on the shoulders of the primary caregiver. Yet, in the spirit of community and shared support, this chapter opens the door to a broader, more inclusive approach to caregiving. "Delegating to Friends, Family, Church, and Community Groups" explores the invaluable role of a diverse support network in enhancing the care of aging parents. From the warmth of familiar faces to the helping hands of community organizations, this chapter delves into how to weave a tapestry of care that extends beyond professional assistance.

Key Points

1. **The Power of a Multi-Faceted Support Network.** Understanding the benefits of involving friends, family, and community groups in caregiving.

2. **Tapping Into Emotional and Spiritual Support.** Leveraging the unique emotional and spiritual support that personal connections and faith-based communities offer.

3. **Community Resources as Pillars of Support.** Utilizing services like Meals on Wheels and senior activity groups for additional care and social interaction.

4. **Strategies for Effective Delegation.** Practical tips on assessing needs, communicating clearly, and showing appreciation to ensure successful task delegation.

Learning Objectives

- Recognize the Value of a Diverse Support Network. Learn the importance of expanding your caregiving network beyond professional caregivers to include personal and community connections.
- Identify Potential Sources of Support. Gain insights into how to

identify and engage friends, family, church members, and community organizations in caregiving.

- Master the Art of Delegation. Develop skills to delegate caregiving tasks effectively, ensuring that each member of your support network contributes in a way that aligns with their strengths and availability.
- Maintain and Strengthen Your Support Network. Understand strategies to keep your network engaged and appreciated, fostering a sustainable and supportive caregiving environment.

Chapter 9:
Delegating to Friends, Family, Church, and Community Groups

The Importance of a Support Network

While professional caregivers play a crucial role in your parent's well-being, they're just one piece of the puzzle. A robust support network that includes friends, family, church members, and community groups can provide additional layers of care and companionship. This network can also give you, the primary caregiver, some much-needed respite.

Enlisting Your Friends and Family

Friends and family who are close to your parent can offer emotional support that a professional caregiver can't provide. They can visit, engage in social activities, or simply offer a listening ear. Local friends and family can help with grocery shopping, driving your parent to appointments, and other errands.

For many seniors, spiritual well-being is just as important as physical health. Members of your parent's church or spiritual group can visit, offer companionship, and sometimes even assist with practical needs.

Many churches have outreach programs specifically designed to assist seniors. These can include meal delivery, home visits, and recreational activities. For more information about how to galvanize a faith-based organization around your parent or a loved one, see my ***Eldercare 180° program at the end of this book***. Organizations like Meals on Wheels not only deliver food but also offer an opportunity for social interaction. In addition, local community centers often have senior activity groups that can provide social interaction and mental stimulation.

How to Delegate Effectively

First, **Assess Needs and Availability**. Before you start delegating tasks, understand what needs to be done and who is available to help. Not everyone will have the same amount of time or the same skills to offer. Second, **Clear Communication**. Be specific about what you're asking for. Instead of saying,

"Can you help with mom?", say, "Can you take mom to her doctor's appointment next Friday?" Third, **Show Appreciation**. Always express gratitude to those who help out. A simple thank you can go a long way in maintaining a strong support network.

Action Plan

1. **Expand Your Network**. In addition to researching local resources and hiring caregivers, reach out to friends, family, and community organizations that can offer support.

2. **Delegate Wisely.** Use the tips for effective delegation to assign tasks to your support network.

3. **Maintain the Network**. Keep lines of communication open and express your appreciation regularly to keep your support network strong and engaged.

Conclusion

Building a comprehensive care team for your aging parent involves more than just hiring a professional caregiver. It's about creating a robust support network that includes healthcare providers, friends, family, and community resources. By doing so, you not only ensure a higher quality of life for your parent but also share the caregiving burden with others who care.

Remember, it takes a village to provide the best care for your aging parent, especially when you're managing it from a distance. With the right team in place, you can face the challenges of remote eldercare with confidence and peace of mind.

Chapter 10 Introduction: Eldercare Communication Strategies

Executive Summary

Welcome to Chapter 10, a pivotal section of Part II. If you're an Adult Child of an Aging Parent (ACAP), you already know that communication is the backbone of effective caregiving. But let's face it, talking about sensitive issues like health, finances, and long-term care can be a minefield, especially when you're not physically there. This chapter aims to arm you with practical strategies for two critical communication channels: one with your aging parents and the other with your siblings and extended family.

Key Points

- **Effective Communication with Aging Parents**. Learn how to navigate the often tricky conversations about health, finances, and future planning with your parents. We'll cover how to approach these topics sensitively, ensuring that your parents feel respected and involved in their own care.

- **Coordinating with Siblings and Extended Family**. If you've ever felt like you're carrying the weight of your parent's care on your shoulders, this section is for you. We'll delve into how to effectively coordinate responsibilities and communicate with your siblings and extended family to ensure everyone is on the same page.

Learning Objectives

1. Understand the nuances of communicating with aging parents about sensitive topics, including how to initiate conversations and what language to use.

2. Gain actionable strategies for coordinating care responsibilities with siblings and extended family, including how to divide tasks and make collective decisions.

Communication is more than just talking; it's about making connections, fostering understanding, and building a support system. As an ACAP, you're juggling your own life and responsibilities while also worrying about your aging parents. It's a tough balancing act, and clear, compassionate communication can make all the difference. This chapter will give you the tools you need to navigate these complex dynamics, making the caregiving journey smoother for everyone involved.

Chapter 10:
Eldercare Communication Strategies

You've made it to Chapter 10, and if you're here, it's because you're committed to providing the best possible care for your aging parents. As an Adult Child of an Aging Parent (ACAP), you're in a unique position. You're not just a caregiver; you're also a son, daughter, or perhaps even a grandchild.

This dual role can make communication especially challenging. In this chapter, we'll explore how to navigate these complex dynamics effectively.

Effective Communication with Aging Parents

Communication is the cornerstone of any relationship, but when it comes to your aging parents, it takes on a new level of importance. You're not just sharing news or making plans for a family dinner; you're discussing their health, their independence, and their future. Let's be real for a minute. Initiating a conversation about eldercare with your aging parent is a big deal. It's not like discussing the weather or the latest family gossip.

You're venturing into sensitive territory that touches on issues of independence, vulnerability, and the passage of time. As an ACAP, you might be dreading this conversation, worried about saying the wrong thing or triggering an emotional response. Trust me, you're not alone in feeling this way.

Timing is everything—avoid holidays or family gatherings. As tempting as it might be to bring everyone into one room and hash it out, family gatherings are emotionally charged events. Stick to a more neutral time. This isn't a conversation to squeeze into a 15-minute window. Make sure both you and your parent have ample time to talk—and listen.

Before you even utter the first word, think about the environment. Is it conducive to a serious conversation? Make sure the setting is comfortable for your parent. If they have a favorite chair or a spot in the house where they like to sit, aim to have the conversation there. Eliminate distractions—turn off the TV, put away phones, and make sure you won't be interrupted. The focus should be solely on the conversation at hand.

How do you even start a conversation like this? Here's a tip: be straightforward but gentle. You might say something like, "Mom/Dad, I think it's time we discuss your living situation and what kind of help you might need." Be Direct but Tactful—There's no point dancing around the subject, but you also don't want to be so blunt that you cause distress.

Use "I" Statements—frame the conversation in terms of your own concerns and observations. This can make the discussion feel less like an attack on their independence. For example, "I've noticed you're having some difficulty with chores around the house."

Let's face it; this conversation is fraught with emotional landmines. Your parent might react with denial, anger, or even sadness. Be prepared for resistance—understand that your parent might not be ready to accept that they need help. And that's okay. The important thing is that you've initiated the conversation. Show empathy. Put yourself in their shoes. How would you feel if someone were discussing your ability to take care of yourself? Acknowledge their feelings and reassure them that the goal is to make life easier and safer for them.

You've laid it all out on the table. Now what? Before ending the conversation, summarize what was discussed and what the next steps are. This ensures everyone is on the same page. Make it clear that this is an ongoing conversation. As circumstances change, you'll need to revisit and revise the care plan.

The conversation about eldercare is not a one-and-done deal. It's the beginning of an ongoing dialogue that will evolve over time. But initiating that first conversation is a crucial step.

It sets the stage for open communication and collaborative planning, making the challenging journey of caregiving just a little bit easier for everyone involved.

Coordinating with Siblings and Extended Family

Let's not sugarcoat it—family dynamics can be complicated. As an ACAP, you're not just dealing with the logistics of caregiving; you're also navigating a labyrinth of family relationships, past grievances, and differing opinions—to say the least. It's a lot to handle, and it's why a structured approach to coordinating with siblings and extended family is so crucial.

If you've ever felt like you're the only one taking on the brunt of caregiving responsibilities, you're not alone. It's a common sentiment among ACAPs, and it can lead to unspoken tensions and resentments within the family. You might find yourself wondering, "Why am I the one doing all the work?" or "Don't they care about Mom and Dad as much as I do?" These are natural feelings, but they can be corrosive if left unaddressed.

The truth is, caregiving is not a solo sport—it's a team endeavor. Your siblings and extended family can offer different perspectives, skills, and resources that you might not have. Sharing the responsibilities can prevent caregiver burnout—a real and serious issue that can affect your health and well-being.

This is a business meeting of sorts, so treat it as such. Send out invitations-make it formal. An email invitation outlining the purpose, agenda, and importance of the meeting can set the right tone. Before the meeting, send out a brief survey to gauge everyone's thoughts on caregiving responsibilities, time commitments, and any specific areas they'd like to handle.

The **initial meeting is more than just a gathering**—it's a **foundational step in your caregiving journey**. It sets the stage for how well (or poorly) the family will work together in caring for your aging parent. Stick to the agenda but be flexible enough to allow for other concerns and questions. Stick to the agenda but be flexible enough to allow for other concerns and questions.

Now comes the nitty-gritty—**dividing up the caregiving tasks**. This is where the pre-meeting survey can be invaluable. Before you can start delegating tasks, you need to know who's capable of what. Make a list of all the tasks that need to be done, and then match them with the skills and strengths of each family member. Maybe your brother is great with finances, while your cousin is a nurse.

Use these skills to your advantage. Of course, you have to be realistic about the time each person can commit. Someone who lives out of state won't be able to handle day-to-day tasks but might be able to manage finances or medical appointments.

Creating a Communications Structure

First, **set your priorities**. What needs to be done **right now**? This could be anything from immediate medical needs to essential home repairs. What are the long-term needs. These are ongoing tasks like bill payments, grocery shopping, and regular medical check-ups. Create an emergency response chain of commend. Who is the first point of contact in case of an emergency? This is often the family member who lives closest to the parent.

Second, **assign roles**. Once you've assessed everyone's strengths and availability, assign roles accordingly. Make sure to get everyone's agreement on their responsibilities. Third, set **deadlines** and **milestones**. I know...I know it sounds 'project management'...*well* it really *is*—one of the most import projects of your life! Ok, back to the task at hand. Determine when will the financial assessment be done? Who is researching care facilities or home care agencies and by when? Fourth, **set up regular family meetings**, whether in-person or via video conferencing.

This can help keep everyone updated and accountable. For quick updates, a family group chat or email thread can be invaluable. I particularly like a tool called Care Bridge, it's a free, private social media platform designed specially for family projects like this.

A weekly email update can keep everyone informed of any changes, issues, or accomplishments. However, you'll probably need monthly meetings for more in-depth discussions, challenges, revising the care plan, and making any necessary changes to responsibilities.

Dealing With Family Drama

Even with the best-laid plans, as I alluded to before, family dynamics can be complicated. And, **conflicts can** and **will arise**. First, having a mechanism for resolving disagreements is essential.

Whether it's a vote or a third-party mediator, decide on a **conflict resolution strategy in advance**. Family drama is totally not productive and will lead to dysfunction.

Second, create an **open forum** where everyone feels comfortable voicing their concerns and disagreements without fear of judgment or backlash. Third, **money matters are often a major source of conflict** in caregiving situations—I know this is a shocker. Transparency is key to preventing misunderstandings and conflicts.

Fourth, use a **shared online spreadsheet** to track all expenses related to caregiving. This ensures transparency and allows for equitable financial contributions.

Fifth, periodically review the finances with all involved to ensure that everyone is contributing as agreed and that funds are being used judiciously.

Conclusion

Coordinating with siblings and extended family is a complex but necessary aspect of caregiving. It requires meticulous planning, open communication, and a fair amount of emotional intelligence. But the payoff is immense: a shared responsibility that lightens the load for everyone and ensures that your aging parent receives the best care possible.

So take the plunge—organize that family meeting, divide those tasks, and set up those communication channels. It's the first step in a collaborative journey that can make the challenging task of caregiving a bit easier for everyone involved.

Chapter 11 Introduction: Eldercare Crisis Management

Executive Summary

Crisis management is an often-overlooked but crucial aspect of managing eldercare from a distance. As Adult Children of Aging Parents (ACAPs), you're not just dealing with the day-to-day logistics of caregiving; you're also the first line of defense in preventing and managing crises.

This chapter aims to equip you with the tools and knowledge to identify red flags and create effective emergency response plans. By being prepared, you can mitigate risks and ensure the safety and well-being of your aging parent, even from afar.

Key Points

- **Identifying Red Flags.** Learn how to recognize the early warning signs of a potential crisis, from sudden changes in behavior to unexplained physical symptoms. Early detection is key to effective crisis management.

- **Emergency Response Plans.** Understand the importance of having a well-thought-out emergency response plan. Know who to call, what to do, and how to coordinate with local caregivers and medical professionals in real-time.

Learning Objectives

1. **Identify Early Warning Signs.** Understand the various red flags that could indicate a looming crisis, whether it's medical, emotional, or environmental.

2. **Create an Emergency Response Plan.** Learn the steps to create a comprehensive emergency response plan that includes contact numbers, medical information, and immediate steps to take in various crisis scenarios.

3. **Coordinate Remote Crisis Management.** Gain insights into leveraging technology and local resources for real-time crisis management.

4. **Communicate Effectively in a Crisis.** Learn how to communicate efficiently with medical professionals, local caregivers, and family members during a crisis.

5. **Review and Update Crisis Plans.** Understand the importance of regularly reviewing and updating your emergency plans to adapt to your aging parent's changing needs.

Chapter 11:
Crisis Management in Remote Eldercare

As Adult Children of Aging Parents (ACAPs), you're already navigating the complexities of remote caregiving. From coordinating medical appointments to ensuring your parent's emotional well-being, you're juggling multiple responsibilities. But what happens when a crisis strikes? Are you prepared to handle it from a distance? This chapter aims to equip you with the tools and knowledge to identify red flags and create effective emergency response plans. By being prepared, you can mitigate risks and ensure the safety and well-being of your aging parent, even from afar.

Identifying Red Flags

A "*red flag*" in eldercare is an early warning sign that something is amiss. You should have a high index of suspicion for these red flags sooner rather than later—ideally start paying closer attention to your parents' habits when they're in their 50s. This gives s baseline. I totally missed this with my parents. It could be a sudden change in your parent's behavior, unexplained physical symptoms, or even a disruption in their daily routine. The key is to recognize these signs early, as they can be indicative of a looming crisis.

Medical Red Flags

First, there's **unexplained weight loss**. For example, Sarah noticed that during her weekly video calls, her mother seemed to be getting thinner. When she asked her mom about it, she shrugged it off, saying she's just not as hungry as she used to be. Concerned, Sarah contacted her mom's primary care physician and arranged for a check-up. It turned out her mother had developed a thyroid issue that was causing the weight loss.

Here's another example, Mark's father always had a healthy appetite. However, during his monthly visits, Mark noticed that his dad's clothes were fitting more loosely. After some probing, his father admitted he had been skipping meals because he was too tired to cook. A medical evaluation revealed early signs of malnutrition.

Second, **there're frequent falls**. Let's say Emily received a call from her father's neighbor saying that he had fallen while taking out the trash. This was the third time in two months. Emily decided it was time to install some safety measures around the house, like grab bars and non-slip mats, and also scheduled a medical check-up for her dad to assess his balance and mobility.

Or let's consider Karen's mother had always been agile, but lately, she had been tripping and falling more often. After the second fall within a month, Karen arranged for a physiotherapist to assess her mother. The assessment revealed that her muscle strength had decreased, increasing her fall risk.

Third, there may be **sudden changes in medication routines**. During a routine call, Lisa's mom casually mentioned that she stopped taking her blood pressure medication because she felt fine. Alarmed, Lisa immediately contacted her mom's doctor, who emphasized the importance of continuing the medication to prevent potential strokes or heart issues.

Paul noticed that the medication reminder app he set up for his father showed multiple missed doses. When questioned, his father said he was feeling better and didn't think the medication was necessary. Paul had to explain that stopping medication abruptly could have severe consequences and got the doctor to reiterate this to his father.

Emotional Red Flags

First, **monitor for withdrawal from social activities**. For example, Jane's mother, who was always the life of the party, suddenly started declining invitations to family gatherings. When Jane probed deeper, her mother admitted feeling overwhelmed and anxious around people, which was a sign of emerging social anxiety.

Tom noticed that his dad, an avid golfer, had not been to the golf course in weeks. When asked, his dad said he just didn't feel like it anymore. This lack of interest in a previously enjoyed activity was a red flag for potential depression.

Second, **watch out for increased irritability**. For instance, Susan found that her usually calm and patient father had started snapping at the smallest things. This change in behavior was not only out of character but also a sign of emotional distress. During their weekly calls, Michelle noticed her mother seemed more irritable and less tolerant of differing opinions. This increased irritability was a red flag that her emotional well-being needed to be assessed.

Environmental Red Flags

First, there's unkempt living conditions. I know, you may be thinking, 'Dr. Walt, may parents could never won in tidiness awards.' Just humor me. For example, during a surprise visit, David found his mother's usually immaculate home in disarray. Dishes were piled up, and the laundry was undone. This was a red flag that she might be struggling with daily chores. When Rachel visited her dad, she noticed that his garden, once his pride and joy, was overgrown and neglected. This signaled that he might be having difficulty maintaining his environment.

Unpaid Bills or Lack of Food In The Home

Mike discovered a stack of unpaid bills and late payment notices when he was helping his mom with her paperwork. This was a red flag that she might be struggling with financial management. During a visit, Emily noticed a utility shut-off notice on her father's kitchen table. When she asked him about it, he seemed confused. This was a red flag indicating potential cognitive decline affecting his ability to manage finances.

Sarah was concerned when she found her dad's fridge nearly empty during a weekend visit. When questioned, he said he hadn't had the energy to go grocery shopping, a red flag for potential physical or emotional issues.

Mark noticed that his mother's pantry was filled with expired food items, and there was a lack of fresh produce. This was a red flag that she might not be eating well, which could lead to nutritional deficiencies. Also, make it a habit to have scheduled calls with your aging parent. These calls can serve as a platform for them to voice any concerns or issues they may be facing. Keep in touch with neighbors or local friends who can provide an "on-the-ground" perspective on your parent's well-being.

Creating an Emergency Response Plan

An **emergency response plan** is your go-to guide for handling crises. It should be comprehensive, easily accessible, and regularly updated. Here's what it should include three important elements: (1) A list of all essential contacts, including doctors, neighbors, and local emergency services. (2) A summary of your parent's medical history, medications, and any known allergies. And, (3) A set of immediate actions to take for different types of crises, such as medical emergencies, falls, or natural disasters.

Leveraging technology in your plan. There are several apps designed to store emergency medical information and contact numbers. Make sure this app is installed on your parent's phone and that local caregivers have access to it. Easily transform you parent's into a **"smart house."** Devices like smart doorbells or home security systems can provide real-time updates on your parent's environment.

Coordinating Crisis Management

In a crisis, **real-time communication is crucial**. Here's how to ensure you're always in the loop. First, **create a family group chat** for immediate updates during a crisis. Second, use video calls for more complex situations where you need to see what's happening. Third, have a **list of local caregivers** who can be on-site in case of an emergency. Fourth, know the **local community resources available**, such as emergency respite care services or local emergency rooms.

Communication do's and don'ts during a crisis. Do be **clear** and **concise**. In a crisis, time is of the essence. Be clear and concise in your communication. **Don't panic**. It's easier said than done, but panicking can cloud your judgment and lead to poor decision-making.

Assign one family member to communicate with medical professionals. This ensures that the information is consistent and centralized. Keep a record of all medical advice and instructions. This can be crucial for follow-up care and for keeping all family members informed.

Crisis plans are not a "set it and forget it" affair. You need to review and updated them regularly to adapt to your aging parent's changing needs. Make it a point to review the emergency response plan every three months. After any crisis, review what went well and what didn't. Use these insights to update your plan.

Action Plan

1. **Identify Potential Red Flags**. Start by making a list of potential red flags specific to your parent's situation.

2. **Create an Emergency Response Plan**. Use the guidelines provided to create a comprehensive emergency response plan.

3. **Set Up Communication Channels**. Establish how you will communicate with family members and local caregivers in case of a crisis.

4. **Conduct a Mock Drill**. Run a mock crisis drill to test the effectiveness of your plan and communication channels.

Conclusion

Crisis management is an integral part of remote eldercare. While we all hope that a crisis never occurs, the reality is that it's always a possibility. Being unprepared is not an option. By identifying red flags early and having a well-thought-out emergency response plan, you can ensure that you're doing everything in your power to keep your aging parent safe and well-cared-for, even from a distance.

Being an ACAP is challenging, but it's also an opportunity to provide your aging parent with the love, care, and dignity they deserve in their twilight years. So take the time to prepare for the unexpected—it's the best way to show your love.

Overview of Part III
Aging in Place

Executive Summary

Part III, "Aging in Place," delves into the strategies and resources required to help your aging parents continue living in their own homes safely and comfortably. This section is particularly relevant for those who prefer community-based care over institutional settings for their loved ones.

Key Points:

1. **Home Modifications for Safety and Comfort**

This chapter outlines the necessary home adjustments to ensure a safe and comfortable living environment for your aging parent.

2. **Community Resources for Aging in Place**

Local community resources can be invaluable. This chapter guides you through identifying and leveraging these resources for your parent's benefit.

3. **Health and Wellness**

Maintaining good health is crucial for aging in place. This chapter focuses on nutrition, exercise, and other wellness factors tailored for the elderly.

4. **Social and Emotional Well-being**

Loneliness can be a significant issue for aging parents. This chapter offers strategies to keep your parent socially engaged and emotionally healthy.

Learning Objectives:

- Understand the importance of home modifications and learn how to implement them effectively.
- Become knowledgeable about community resources that can aid in aging in place.
- Gain insights into maintaining the physical health and emotional well-being of your aging parent.
- Develop a comprehensive plan that integrates all aspects of aging in place, from home safety to social engagement.

Action Plan:

1. Home Safety Audit

Conduct a thorough safety audit of your parent's home using the checklist provided. Identify areas that need modification or improvement.

2. Resource Mapping

Create a map of local resources, such as community centers, healthcare providers,

and grocery delivery services. Make initial contact and understand how they can assist your parent.

3. Wellness Plan

Develop a wellness plan that includes a balanced diet, exercise routine, and regular medical check-ups. Discuss and finalize this plan with your parent and their healthcare provider.

4. Social Engagement Calendar

Create a monthly calendar of social activities for your parent. This could include

community events, family visits, and virtual meet-ups.

5. Emergency Contacts List

Compile a list of emergency contacts, including neighbors, local emergency services, and healthcare providers. Make this list easily accessible to your parent.

6. Periodic Review

Every quarter, review the effectiveness of your aging-in-place plan. Make necessary adjustments based on your parent's changing needs and consult the book for additional guidance. By following this action plan, you'll create a supportive environment that allows your aging parent to maintain their independence while ensuring their safety and well-being.

Chapter 12 Introduction: Home Safety for Aging in Place

Executive Summary

This chapter, guided by a gerontologist's insights, focuses on key modifications to make homes safer and more comfortable for seniors aging in place. Emphasizing the significance of the bathroom as a high-risk area for accidents, the chapter provides practical advice for transforming various areas of the home into safe, accessible, and inviting spaces.

Key Points

1. **Welcoming Entryways.** Discusses the importance of creating safe, accessible entryways and provides tips on lighting, decluttering, and modifying door handles.

2. **Stairs.** Offers strategies for making stairs safer, including the installation of dual railings, stairlifts, ramps, and visual aids for step edges.

3. **Bathrooms.** Focuses on the bathroom as a critical area for safety interventions, covering non-slip flooring, grab bars, accessible bathing options, and raised toilet

seats.

4. **Kitchens.** Addresses modifications to make kitchens safer and more accessible, such as lowering shelves, installing safe appliances, and ensuring spacious navigation.

5. **Living Spaces.** Provides suggestions for arranging living spaces for comfort and safety, emphasizing furniture placement, adequate lighting, and emergency response systems.

Learning Objectives

- **Enhancing Home Safety.** Learn how to assess and improve the safety of different areas in a senior's home, with a special focus on high-risk areas like bathrooms.
- **Practical Modification Strategies.** Gain practical knowledge on how

to implement home modifications that enhance both safety and independence for seniors.

- **Balancing Aesthetics and Functionality.** Understand how to maintain a balance between creating a safe environment and preserving the aesthetic and comfort of the home.

- **Empowering Seniors Through Design.** Learn how thoughtful home modifications can empower seniors, allowing them to thrive in their familiar environment with dignity.

Action Plan

1. **Home Safety Assessment.** Steps to evaluate each area of the home for potential risks and necessary modifications.

2. **Implementing Modifications.** Guidelines on prioritizing and executing changes to enhance safety and accessibility.

3. **Ongoing Adaptation.** Advice on continuously adapting the living space to meet the evolving needs of aging seniors.

Chapter 12:
Home Safety for Aging in Place

As a gerontologist, I have witnessed how the transformation of living spaces into safe havens can significantly uplift the quality of life for our elders. Aging gracefully at home requires thoughtful modifications, turning everyday environments into sanctuaries of safety and comfort. In this chapter, we'll explore key areas in the home, with a special focus on the bathroom, which is often the most vulnerable spot for accidents in a senior's home.

Bathrooms-Sanctuary And Safety

In the realm of home safety, the bathroom demands our utmost attention. Research from Canada highlights that **falls in the bathroom are more likely to result in severe injuries** compared to other rooms. Activities like **transferring, ambulation, and standing**, compounded by factors such as slipping, misjudged behavior, and health issues, make the bathroom a critical area for safety interventions.

To create a bathroom that is both a sanctuary and a safe space, **non-slip flooring is essential to prevent dangerous slips.** Imagine the peace of mind that comes from knowing a loved one is less likely to fall on a secure surface. Supportive grab bars, strategically placed near the toilet and in the shower, offer stability during transitions, acting as steadfast aides in daily routines.

For bathing, consider the benefits of **walk-in tubs or showers** equipped with benches and handheld shower-heads, transforming the simple act of bathing into an experience that is not just safe, but also enjoyable. **Elevated toilet seats** with arms can significantly enhance comfort and independence, preserving the dignity of our elders. Take the case of Mr. Lee, who, after a frightening fall, had his bathroom transformed with these modifications, instilling in him a newfound confidence and security.

Welcoming Entryways

Transitioning to entryways, we recognize their role as the first line of defense in home safety. Bright, **motion-activated lights** can prevent stumbles and falls, guiding the way like silent guardians. A clutter-free entryway, free from tripping hazards like loose rugs or unnecessary decorations, is not just aesthetically pleasing but crucial for safety. **Lever-style door handles** are a small change with a profound impact, especially helpful for those with arthritis. Consider Mrs. Thompson, who enjoys her evening garden walks. A motion-sensor light by her front door now gently guides her back inside, ensuring her safety and independence.

Steps to Stair Safety

Stairs in a home can pose a **significant challenge for your parents' mobility**. **Dual railings** on staircases offer a sturdy grip, a simple yet effective aid in navigating between floors. For homes with multiple levels, the installation of stairlifts or ramps can be life-changing, especially for those with mobility challenges. Visible steps, marked with contrasting colors on the edges, can significantly reduce the risk of missteps. Mr. Patel's story is a testament to this; his cherished upstairs library became accessible again with the installation of a **stairlift**, renewing his freedom and joy in his home. My parents live in a traditional two-story house with steep stairs. We had a stairlift installed for them—it was definitely a game changer for them.

Kitchens

In the kitchen, the heart of the home, safety and accessibility are key. Lowering shelves and using pull-out drawers can rekindle the joy of cooking, making essential items easily accessible. Safe appliances with automatic shut-off features and simple controls can prevent accidents, ensuring a secure cooking environment. Spacious navigation is crucial, particularly for those using walkers or wheelchairs. Mrs. Gomez, a wheelchair user, found renewed delight in her passion for cooking with her kitchen's transformation to accommodate her needs.

Living Spaces

In living spaces, thoughtful furniture placement can create an environment that is both elegant and safe. Open, clear pathways and the removal of low-lying obstacles are essential for easy navigation. Good lighting plays a dual role in these spaces - ensuring visibility and creating a warm, inviting ambiance. An emergency response system can provide peace of mind, offering quick assistance at the press of a button. Mr. Smith's living room transformation, with its open spaces and bright lights, is a perfect example of how these modifications not only ensure safety but also uplift the spirit.

Conclusion

Our goal is to weave safety seamlessly into the fabric of everyday living. These thoughtful modifications are not just about preventing accidents—they're about honoring independence and dignity.

Chapter 13 Introduction:
Community Resources for Aging in Place

Executive Summary

Chapter 13 opens the door to a world where the community becomes an integral part of the eldercare journey. This chapter delves into the myriad of local resources that can be harnessed to enrich the lives of aging parents. From volunteer programs in small towns to senior-focused activities in urban community centers, this chapter reveals how these resources serve as extensions of family care, offering support, companionship, and a sense of belonging.

Key Points

1. **Creating a Supportive Ecosystem.** Understanding how community programs and volunteer initiatives can supplement family care.

2. **Navigating Local Offerings.** Discovering and utilizing hidden gems in community resources, such as senior-focused activities and services.

3. **Building Bridges.** Encouraging aging parents to engage with local groups and clubs to foster social connections and community involvement.

4. **Accessible Health Care Options.** Exploring various local health care services, including mobile health clinics, telemedicine, and community health workshops, and their impact on seniors' well-being.

5. **Social Engagement Opportunities.** Highlighting the importance of social activities like art classes, gardening projects, and tech clubs in enhancing seniors' quality of life.

Learning Objectives

- **Identify and Leverage Community Resources.** Equip readers with the knowledge to find and effectively utilize local services and programs for aging parents.
- **Foster Social and Community Engagement.** Understand the importance of social connections in aging and learn strategies to

encourage parents to participate in community activities.

- **Navigate Health Care Options**. Gain insights into local health care services that are accessible and beneficial for aging parents.
- **Cultivate a Holistic Support Network**. Recognize the value of building a robust network that includes not just family but also friends, community members, and professional caregivers.

Action Plan

1. **Community Resource Exploration**. Steps to identify and connect with potential community resources and services.

2. **Encouraging Parental Participation**. Tactics for motivating aging parents to become involved in community groups and activities.

3. **Health Care Navigation**. Guidelines on how to access and utilize local health care services for seniors.

This chapter serves as a guide for Adult Children of Aging Parents (ACAPs) to embrace the wealth of resources available in their communities. It highlights how integrating these resources into the eldercare plan not only eases the caregiving burden but also enriches the lives of their aging parents. By tapping into local offerings and fostering community engagement, ACAPs can ensure their parents enjoy a fuller, more connected life as they age in place.

Chapter 13:
Community Resources for Aging in Place

The community acts as an extended family, offering a network of care and support. For instance, in a small town in Oregon, a community program pairs seniors with local volunteers who assist with everything from grocery shopping to yard maintenance, fostering a sense of belonging and mutual care.

ACAPs can start by visiting local community centers or libraries where bulletin boards often list various senior-focused activities and services. For example, a community in Florida offers a weekly senior yoga class in the park, promoting both physical health and social interaction. Encourage your parents to join local groups or clubs. In a community in Michigan, a book club for seniors led to the formation of a tight-knit group that regularly meets for discussions, fostering deep connections and a sense of community.

Accessible Health Care Options

In the journey of aging in place, ensuring accessible health care is paramount. In **rural areas or communities** where transportation is a challenge, mobile health clinics have become a game-changer. For instance, in a remote community in Montana, a mobile clinic visits every fortnight, offering check-ups, vaccinations, and basic medical services right at the seniors' doorsteps. This service is particularly beneficial for those with mobility issues or chronic conditions that require regular monitoring.

The mobile clinic not only provides essential health services but also reduces the stress and difficulty associated with traveling to distant medical facilities. It ensures that seniors receive timely medical attention, which is crucial for maintaining their overall health and well-being.

With the advent of technology, telemedicine has become increasingly popular, especially in the context of eldercare. A community in Arizona has implemented a telemedicine program where seniors can consult with healthcare professionals via video calls. This service is particularly useful for routine follow-ups or non-emergency medical queries. Telemedicine offers convenience and immediate access to healthcare professionals, which is invaluable for seniors who may find it challenging to leave their homes frequently. It also provides a sense of security, knowing that medical advice is just a call away.

Preventive health care is as important as treating existing conditions. In a **suburban neighborhood** near Chicago, the local community center organizes regular health workshops focusing on topics relevant to seniors, such as nutrition, exercise, mental health, and chronic disease management.

These workshops not only educate seniors about maintaining their health but also provide a platform for social interaction. Seniors get an opportunity to meet peers, share experiences, and learn in a supportive environment. Additionally, these workshops often connect seniors with local health resources and professionals, further integrating them into a network of care.

The Joy of Togetherness

Social engagement plays a critical role in the well-being of seniors, offering not just entertainment but also vital connections to the community and a sense of purpose. This section explores various avenues for social engagement, providing real-world examples to illustrate their impact.

For instance, in a vibrant community in Santa Fe, New Mexico, a local art studio offers weekly painting classes specifically designed for seniors. These classes are not just about learning art; they are a hub for creativity, relaxation, and socialization. Seniors work on various projects, from watercolor painting to pottery, in a supportive and inspiring environment. Participants not only develop their artistic skills but also form meaningful friendships. The classes provide a sense of accomplishment and a creative outlet, which are essential for mental health. The art studio becomes a place where seniors can express themselves freely and feel valued.

In a small town in Oregon, a community garden has become a gathering spot for seniors. They tend to individual plots where they grow vegetables, herbs, and flowers. The garden also hosts weekly gatherings where participants share gardening tips, enjoy fresh produce, and engage in friendly conversations.

The community garden offers physical activity, fresh air, and a sense of achievement as seniors see their plants grow. It fosters a sense of community as they work together, share experiences, and support each other. The garden becomes a natural setting for social interaction and building a support network.

Another strategy is recognizing the growing importance of technology, a community center in Toronto has started a 'Senior Tech Club.' Here, seniors learn to use smartphones, tablets, and computers. The club also explores social media, helping seniors connect with family and friends online. Additionally, they hold regular sessions on internet safety and digital literacy.

The tech club empowers seniors by making them more tech-savvy, enabling them to stay connected with loved ones and access online resources. It also provides a platform for intergenerational interaction, as younger volunteers often come in to assist and teach, fostering mutual respect and understanding between generations.

Let's Consider Transportation Services

Accessible transportation is a cornerstone of independence for seniors, especially for those choosing to age in place. This section delves into volunteer driver programs, special transit services, and senior-friendly ride-share apps.

In a close-knit community in Vermont, a **volunteer driver program** has been established where local volunteers use their own vehicles to transport seniors to appointments, grocery stores, and social events. This service is particularly beneficial for those who no longer drive and live in areas with limited public transportation. The program not only provides a practical solution to mobility challenges but also fosters a sense of community. Seniors feel more connected and less isolated, knowing they have reliable and friendly transportation assistance. It also offers an opportunity for intergenerational interaction and strengthens community ties.

A city in California has implemented a **specialized transit service** for seniors and individuals with disabilities. These services include door-to-door transportation with vehicles equipped to handle mobility aids. The service operates throughout the city and its suburbs, ensuring that seniors can travel safely to their destinations.

This dedicated transit service provides seniors with the freedom to attend medical appointments, visit friends, or engage in community activities without relying on family or friends. It ensures safe and comfortable travel, accommodating the specific needs of each individual, thus promoting their independence and quality of life.

In response to the **growing tech-savvy senior population**, a ride-sharing company has introduced senior-friendly features in its app. These features include larger text, simplified navigation, and the option to request assistance for seniors during the ride. The service is available in a metropolitan area, offering an alternative to traditional taxi services.

The adapted ride-sharing service provides a convenient and modern solution for seniors who are comfortable with smartphones. It offers flexibility and immediacy, allowing seniors to plan trips on short notice. The additional features ensure that the service is accessible and user-friendly for the elderly, aligning with their comfort and needs.

Let's Turn Our Attention to Nutritional Support

Proper nutrition is fundamental for the health and well-being of seniors, particularly for those aging in place. In his section we'll explore various nutritional support programs and services designed to meet the dietary needs of the elderly, along with examples that illustrate their importance and impact. In a suburban community in Texas, the local **Meals on Wheels program** delivers nutritious, freshly prepared meals to seniors who are homebound or unable to cook for themselves. The program caters to dietary restrictions and preferences, ensuring that each senior receives meals that are not only healthy but also enjoyable.

This service does more than just provide food; it offers a lifeline of nourishment and care. The daily visits by volunteers also serve as a wellness check and a source of social interaction, which can be crucial for seniors living alone. The program ensures that seniors have access to balanced meals, contributing to their overall health and enabling them to age in place with dignity.

In Mooresville, North Carolina the Charles Mack **Senior Center Community Center** hosts a senior nutrition program where seniors can gather for a communal lunch. The center offers a variety of healthy meal options, along with nutrition education sessions and cooking demonstrations tailored to the needs of older adults.

The nutrition center becomes more than a place to eat; it's a social hub where seniors can connect with peers, share stories, and enjoy a sense of community. The educational aspect of the program empowers seniors with knowledge about healthy eating habits, addressing nutritional challenges that come with aging.

In an urban area in New York, a **grocery assistance program** partners with local supermarkets to provide grocery delivery services to seniors. Volunteers assist with shopping, ensuring that seniors can access fresh and healthy food choices. The program also offers nutritional counseling to help seniors make informed food choices. This service provides a critical link to essential nutrition for seniors who may find it challenging to go grocery shopping due to mobility issues or health concerns. It not only ensures that they have access to fresh ingredients but also respects their autonomy in making their own food choices, thereby maintaining their independence and quality of life.

Educational and Recreational Programs

Local libraries or community colleges often offer classes tailored to seniors. In a community in Colorado, a series of history lectures geared towards seniors has become a popular weekly event, combining education with social engagement. Many seniors find joy in giving back. In a city in Illinois, a group of seniors' volunteers at the local animal shelter, providing care to animals while enjoying the emotional benefits of companionship. Community resource mapping is another strategy to engage community resources. This action plan includes identifying local resources, contacting organizations for information, and even visiting sites to assess their suitability and accessibility for your aging parents.

Building a Support Network

For seniors aging in place, a robust support network is essential for their well-being and independence. This section focuses on the importance of building a circle of care, encompassing family, friends, community members, and professional caregivers. Let's take a look at neighborhood support groups, family care coordination, and volunteer buddy programs.

For examples, in a close-knit neighborhood in Oregon, residents have formed a **support group for the elderly in their community.** This group organizes regular check-ins, social gatherings, and assistance with daily tasks for seniors. Neighbors take turns visiting the elderly, helping with grocery shopping, or simply spending time with them. This neighborhood initiative fosters a sense of belonging and security among the elderly. It ensures that seniors have a network of people they can rely on for both practical help and social interaction. The regular engagement with neighbors helps to reduce feelings of isolation and promotes a supportive community environment.

A family in Florida has created a **coordinated care plan** for their aging parent. They use a shared online calendar to schedule visits, medical appointments, and other necessary tasks. Each family member contributes according to their ability, whether it's providing transportation, managing finances, or simply spending quality time.

This approach ensures that the senior family member receives consistent care and attention from loved ones. It also helps to distribute the responsibilities among family members, preventing caregiver burnout. The senior feels supported and valued, maintaining strong family bonds.

A church in Charlotte, North Carolina runs my **Eldercare 180° Program where** specially-trained **teams of volunteers are paired with seniors** in the community. These volunteers regularly visit their senior buddies, help them around the house, engage in recreational activities, transport and accompany them to appointments, and provide companionship.

The program creates meaningful connections between seniors and other community members. It provides seniors with a sense of companionship and belonging, reducing feelings of loneliness. This provides Adult Children of Aging Parents a much-needed break and peace of mind. The volunteers, often younger individuals or peers, gain a sense of purpose and fulfillment from helping others, fostering intergenerational relationships.

Engagement Strategies and Inspiring Participation

Engagement strategies are crucial for encouraging seniors to participate actively in their communities and maintain a sense of purpose and connection. This section delves into various methods and programs designed to inspire participation among seniors aging in place. Let's consider senior-focused workshops, intergenerational programs, and senior fitness and health and wellness programs.

For example, in a mid-sized city in Virginia, a local **community college offers a series of educational workshops** specifically designed for seniors. These workshops cover a range of topics, from technology literacy to creative arts and local history. The classes are tailored to be senior-friendly, with a focus on interactive and collaborative learning.

These workshops provide seniors with opportunities to learn new skills, engage their minds, and interact with peers who share similar interests. The educational setting fosters a sense of achievement and mental stimulation, which is vital for cognitive health. Additionally, it offers a platform for social interaction, helping to combat loneliness and isolation.

A community center in Colorado has initiated an **intergenerational program** where seniors collaborate with local youth groups on various projects, such as community gardening, storytelling sessions, and cultural exchange activities. These programs bring together different generations, fostering mutual understanding and respect. Intergenerational engagement breaks down age barriers and stereotypes, creating a more inclusive community. Seniors benefit from the fresh perspectives and energy of the younger participants, while the youth gain wisdom and experience from their elder counterparts. This exchange enriches the lives of both groups and strengthens community bonds.

In a coastal town in California, a **fitness center has developed a series of wellness clubs specifically for seniors.** These clubs offer activities like yoga, water aerobics, and walking groups, all tailored to the fitness levels and needs of older adults. The clubs also incorporate social events and health education sessions. These wellness clubs provide seniors with a supportive environment to maintain physical health and mobility. The group setting encourages regular participation and fosters a sense of camaraderie among members. The inclusion of social and educational components addresses the holistic well-being of seniors, promoting both physical and mental health.

Action Plan

1. **Community Resource Mapping**. Step-by-step guidance on how to locate and connect with local services and programs.

2. **Building a Support Network. Tips** on creating a network of community-based support, including family, friends, and local organizations.

3. **Engagement Strategies**. Practical advice on encouraging seniors to participate in community activities and programs.

Conclusion

Incorporating community resources into the aging-in-place plan can significantly enhance the quality of life for seniors. By tapping into these local treasures, ACAPs can ensure their aging parents not only live safely and comfortably but also remain connected, active, and fulfilled within their community.

Chapter 14 Introduction: Health and Wellness

Executive Summary

"Health and Wellness," zeroes in on the crucial aspect of sustaining a healthy lifestyle for seniors, especially those aging in place. This chapter is a holistic exploration into the realm of health and wellness for the elderly. It delves deep into nutrition and meal planning, coupled with effective exercise and mobility strategies, equipping caregivers with essential insights and techniques to ensure their aging relatives enjoy a fulfilling and high-quality life.

Key Points

1. **Nutrition and Aging.** Examining the evolving nutritional needs of seniors, emphasizing the importance of a well-balanced diet for maintaining health.

2. **Dietary Challenges and Solutions.** Addressing common issues like appetite changes and eating habits, while providing practical solutions to these challenges.

3. **Diet and Chronic Conditions.** Understanding the crucial role of diet in managing common chronic conditions in older adults, and how food interacts with medications.

4. **Effective Meal Planning Strategies.** Offering guidance on creating nutritional and appealing meal plans tailored to seniors' preferences and health needs.

5. **Exercise and Mobility for Seniors.** Highlighting the significance of physical activity, focusing on low-impact exercises and adaptations for individuals with mobility limitations.

Learning Objectives

- **Adapt Nutrition to Aging Needs.** Learn to modify dietary choices to meet the unique nutritional requirements and tastes of the elderly.
- **Overcome Dietary Challenges.** Develop strategies to tackle common issues like reduced appetite or difficulties in chewing and

swallowing.

- **Incorporate Diet in Chronic Disease Management**. Gain an understanding of how dietary adjustments can manage and improve health conditions.
- **Plan and Prepare Nutritious Meals**. Acquire the skills for effective meal planning and preparation, keeping in mind special dietary needs and preferences.
- **Encourage Appropriate Physical Activity**. Gain knowledge of suitable exercises for the elderly, considering their fitness levels and mobility limitations, to maintain overall health and well-being.

This chapter stands as an essential guide for caregivers and families, underlining the interconnection between nutrition and exercise in the wellness of seniors. By comprehending these fundamental elements and applying the outlined strategies, caregivers can significantly enhance the health, happiness, and overall quality of life for their aging loved ones. The focus is not merely on longevity but on ensuring a vibrant, joyous, and fulfilling life in their golden years.

Chapter 14:

Health and Wellness

Aging gracefully and healthily is a goal we all have for our loved ones. As they enter their golden years, the focus on health and wellness becomes more critical, especially when they are aging in place.

This chapter is dedicated to unraveling the complexities of maintaining a healthy lifestyle in the elderly, with a particular focus on nutrition and meal planning, alongside exercise and mobility. Through practical guidance and effective strategies, we aim to empower caregivers and families in ensuring that their aging relatives enjoy a high quality of life.

The Importance of Nutrition in Aging—A Delicate Balance

As our loved one's age, their bodies undergo significant changes that affect their nutritional needs. Metabolism slows down, the sense of taste and smell might diminish, and they may face difficulties in chewing or digesting food. These changes necessitate a closer look at their diet to ensure they are receiving the proper nutrients. It's not just about eating; it's about eating right. For example, calcium and vitamin D become more critical for maintaining bone health, while fiber is essential for digestive health.

One of the most significant challenges in eldercare is dealing with changes in appetite and eating habits. Many elderly individuals experience a reduced appetite, which can lead to unintentional weight loss and nutritional deficiencies. To combat this, it's important to focus on nutrient-dense foods that provide the necessary vitamins and minerals in smaller portions.

Preparing visually appealing and flavorful meals can also stimulate appetite. For those with difficulty chewing or swallowing, modifying food textures can make a significant difference, such as opting for soft-cooked vegetables or ground meats.

Many elderly individuals manage chronic conditions like diabetes, heart disease, or osteoporosis, where diet plays a crucial role. Tailoring their meals to accommodate these conditions can help manage and sometimes improve their health. It's also vital to be aware of how certain foods interact with medications. For instance, grapefruit can interfere with the effectiveness of some blood pressure medications, while foods high in vitamin K can affect blood thinners.

Strategies for Effective Meal Planning

Creating a balanced and appealing meal plan for the elderly requires understanding their nutritional needs and preferences. It's about striking a balance between the necessary nutrients and the foods they enjoy. Incorporating a variety of fruits, vegetables, whole grains, lean proteins, and dairy ensures they receive a wide range of nutrients. Special dietary needs, whether due to allergies, intolerances, or chronic conditions, should be considered in meal planning.

Leveraging resources like meal delivery services can be a boon for those unable to prepare meals. These services offer nutritionally balanced meals, tailored to dietary needs, and delivered right to their door. Additionally, community programs often provide meal support and social opportunities, which can be especially beneficial for those living alone.

Exercise and Mobility in the Elderly

Regular physical activity is essential for maintaining health in the elderly. It not only improves physical health but also has a positive impact on mental well-being. However, exercise for the elderly should be tailored to their individual fitness levels and any mobility limitations they may have.

Low-impact exercises such as walking, swimming, or yoga can be beneficial without putting undue stress on joints. Strength and flexibility training are also important for maintaining muscle mass and preventing falls.

For those with mobility limitations, exercises can be adapted. For example, chair exercises or light stretching can be effective for those unable to engage in more strenuous activities. It's crucial to use assistive devices as needed to ensure safety during exercise.

Creating a Sustainable Health and Wellness Plan

Integrating nutrition and exercise into the daily life of an elderly individual is key to maintaining their health and wellness. Setting realistic goals and establishing a consistent routine are crucial. This not only helps in maintaining physical health but also provides a sense of structure and purpose.

Caregivers and family members play a vital role in this process. They can provide encouragement, assist in meal preparation, and join in physical activities, making it a shared and enjoyable experience. Educating them about the specific needs and challenges faced by the elderly can enhance their ability to provide effective support.

Regular health check-ups are essential to monitor the effectiveness of the health and wellness plan and to make adjustments as needed. Flexibility is key, as the needs and abilities of the elderly can change over time. By staying attuned to these changes and adapting the plan accordingly.

Conclusion

Through this chapter, we have explored the vital components of maintaining health and wellness in the elderly. A combination of a well-balanced diet and regular physical activity forms the cornerstone of a healthy lifestyle. By understanding and implementing these principles, caregivers and families can significantly enhance the quality of life for their elderly loved ones, ensuring they live happy golden years.

Chapter 15 Introduction: Social and Emotional Well-being

In the twilight years of our parents' lives, we are tasked with a delicate mission that goes beyond attending to their physical health. This mission encompasses nurturing their social and emotional well-being, ensuring that their journey through these years is not only comfortable but also deeply fulfilling. Chapter 15, "Social and Emotional Well-being," delves into the nuanced landscape of our aging parents' emotional and social needs. It aims to shed light on the importance of understanding and combating the loneliness and isolation that can pervade their lives, offering strategies to infuse their days with connection, joy, and a profound sense of belonging.

Executive Summary

This chapter explores the intricate web of social and emotional challenges faced by the elderly, particularly loneliness and isolation, which can often creep in unnoticed following significant life changes. Through a compassionate lens, we examine the symptoms and consequences of these emotional states and propose comprehensive strategies designed to counteract them.

Our goal is to ensure that our parents' golden years are characterized by enriching social interactions, sustained emotional health, and a vibrant engagement with life.

Key Points

1. **The Complexity of Loneliness and Isolation.** Understanding the multifaceted nature of loneliness and isolation in the elderly and their impact on overall well-being.

2. **Identifying Signs of Emotional Distress.** Recognizing the subtle and overt indicators of loneliness, such as withdrawal from social activities and changes in daily routines.

3. **Strategies for Enhancing Social Engagement.** Practical approaches to rekindle social interactions and engagement, including community

participation, the use of technology, and nurturing hobbies.

4. **Cognitive Stimulation for Emotional Health**. Emphasizing the role of mental engagement and cognitive exercises in maintaining emotional balance and mental sharpness.
5. **Addressing Mental Health Proactively**. The importance of recognizing and treating mental health issues such as depression and anxiety with the same seriousness as physical health concerns.

Learning Objectives

- **To Recognize and Address Loneliness and Isolation**. Equip readers with the ability to identify signs of loneliness and isolation in their aging parents and offer effective interventions.
- **To Foster Social and Cognitive Engagement**. Learn strategies to actively involve elderly parents in social, creative, and intellectual pursuits that enrich their emotional lives.
- **To Prioritize and Support Mental Health**. Understand the critical importance of mental health in the elderly and how to approach it with empathy, knowledge, and professional support.

As we navigate the complex emotional landscape of our aging parents, our ultimate aim is to transform their later years into a period of life that is not only lived but truly cherished.

By embracing the strategies outlined in this chapter, we can illuminate their paths with the light of companionship, engagement, and emotional wellness, ensuring they feel valued, loved, and emotionally fulfilled in every moment.

Chapter 15:
Social and Emotional Well-being

Navigating the later years of our parents' lives requires a delicate balance between caring for their physical needs and nurturing their social and emotional well-being. This nuanced journey involves recognizing the subtle shifts in their lifestyle and mood that may signal deeper issues of loneliness and isolation.

As we delve deeper into each topic within this chapter, we aim to offer comprehensive strategies to ensure these years are not only lived but cherished, filled with connection, joy, and fulfillment.

Deepening Understanding of Loneliness and Isolation

Loneliness and isolation in the elderly are **intricate phenomena that quietly infiltrate their lives**, casting long shadows during a period that should be marked by tranquility and fulfillment. Often, these emotional states are precipitated by pivotal life transitions that are inherent to aging, such as the retirement phase, which brings an abrupt end to daily social interactions and a structured routine, or the profound loss of a spouse, friend, or sibling, leaving a void that is difficult to fill.

Such significant changes can disrupt their sense of identity and belonging, leading to feelings of isolation and loneliness.

This sense of disconnection is further exacerbated in **a society where the emotional and social needs of the elderly are not always adequately acknowledged or prioritized**. The bustling pace of modern life, combined with the physical distances that often separate families, can leave our aging population feeling forgotten and sidelined. It is within this context that the signs of loneliness and isolation need to be keenly observed and understood.

These signs are varied and can manifest in both overt and subtle ways. A noticeable withdrawal from previously enjoyed social activities is a clear indicator that something is amiss. This withdrawal may be due to the fear of engaging in a world that seems to have moved on without them or because these activities now evoke feelings of sadness or loss.

Changes in eating or sleeping patterns are also telltale signs of emotional distress. These could range from loss of appetite to overeating, or from insomnia to excessive sleeping, all of which are indicative of an underlying struggle with loneliness or depression.

Furthermore, verbal cues from our loved ones, such as expressions of feeling burdensome to their families or friends, or hints at their perceived lack of value and purpose, are crucial indicators that should not be dismissed as mere ramblings of old age. These expressions are often a silent plea for acknowledgment, understanding, and companionship.

Addressing these signs of loneliness and isolation demands a **proactive and compassionate approach**. It involves creating and fostering environments and opportunities that reignite their sense of belonging and purpose. This can be achieved by encouraging and facilitating their re-engagement with the community, whether through reintroduction to social activities aligned with their interests, support in building new friendships, or simply providing them with spaces where their voices are heard and valued.

The goal is to envelop them in a community that sees beyond their age, recognizing and celebrating their worth, wisdom, and the rich tapestry of experiences they bring to the collective human experience.

In doing so, we not only combat the scourge of loneliness and isolation but also enrich our communities with the depth and diversity of our aging population's contributions.

The path forward involves not just recognition of the problem but active engagement in crafting solutions that bring light and warmth back into the lives of our elderly, ensuring their golden years are lived with dignity, connection, and joy.

Combating Loneliness with Engagement and Technology

Revitalizing our parents' social lives can take many forms, from encouraging participation in community events to leveraging technology to maintain connections. Community engagement provides a sense of belonging and purpose, offering opportunities to meet peers with shared interests or contribute through volunteer work, thus breaking the cycle of isolation.

Meanwhile, technology can serve as a bridge across distances, enabling regular communication with family and friends through video calls or social media, and connecting them with online communities that match their interests.

These digital interactions can supplement real-world interactions, providing a continuous sense of community and support.

Nurturing Hobbies and Intellectual Pursuits

Encouraging our aging parents to pursue hobbies and interests can significantly enhance their emotional well-being. Whether it's through group activities that align with their hobbies, such as knitting circles, cooking classes, or book clubs, or through outings to cultural events that stimulate their minds and senses, these pursuits offer valuable opportunities for social interaction and personal growth. Engaging in these activities helps maintain their cognitive functions and fosters a sense of accomplishment and joy, critical components of a fulfilling life.

Cognitive Stimulation as a Pillar of Emotional Health

Cognitive stimulation stands as a **foundational pillar** in the maintenance of both emotional and mental health, particularly in the later stages of life. As our parents age, engaging in activities that challenge and stimulate the brain becomes **crucial in mitigating the risks of cognitive decline**, which can significantly impact their quality of life and emotional well-being.

Activities such as brain-challenging games, creative outlets, and intellectually stimulating discussions do more than merely serve as sources of entertainment; they are integral components of a holistic approach to eldercare, fostering a state of mental agility that is closely linked with emotional fulfillment.

Brain-challenging games like puzzles, **chess**, Sudoku, or word games offer a fun yet effective way to engage critical thinking and problem-solving skills. These games can sharpen cognitive functions, improving memory, focus, and processing speed.

More importantly, they provide a sense of achievement and joy upon completion, which can be immensely gratifying for our parents, reaffirming their capabilities and resilience against age-related mental challenges.

Creative outlets, on the other hand, offer a different form of cognitive stimulation by encouraging expression, innovation, and emotional exploration. Activities such as painting, writing, crafting, or playing musical instruments allow for personal expression and can be therapeutic.

They serve as channels for communicating thoughts and emotions that might be difficult to articulate in words, thereby enhancing emotional health. The act of creating something new or learning a new skill also boosts self-esteem and fosters a sense of accomplishment and purpose.

Engaging in stimulating discussions and debates about books, current events, history, or personal experiences can be incredibly enriching for the elderly. Such intellectual engagements keep the mind active and encourage lifelong learning, which is vital for cognitive health.

Discussions provide social interaction, reduce feelings of isolation, and stimulate areas of the brain involved in language, reasoning, and memory. They also offer our parents a platform to share their knowledge and wisdom, affirming their value and contributions to the family and broader community.

Encouraging our parents to continue learning and exploring new ideas and hobbies contributes significantly to their overall sense of self-worth and happiness. It reinforces their identity beyond their age, recognizing them as individuals with unique interests, talents, and capabilities.

This acknowledgment is essential for emotional well-being, as it combats stereotypes associated with aging and fosters a more inclusive and respectful view of the elderly.

Incorporating cognitive stimulation into the daily lives of our aging parents is not just about keeping their minds sharp; it's about nurturing their spirits, affirming their value, and enhancing their emotional satisfaction.

By prioritizing activities that stimulate the mind and enrich the soul, we can support our parents in leading more fulfilled, engaged, and joyful lives, even as they navigate the complexities of aging.

Proactively Addressing Mental Health

Proactively addressing mental health in the elderly is a **critical aspect of ensuring their overall well-being**. As our parents age, they may encounter various stressors and changes that can impact their mental health, including the loss of loved ones, physical health issues, and the transition into retirement.

These changes can lead to feelings of depression, anxiety, and isolation if not addressed properly. It is essential to recognize that mental health issues are not an inevitable part of aging and that our parents deserve the same level of care and attention to their mental health as they do to their physical health.

Early recognition of mental health issues is key to preventing their escalation. Signs such as persistent sadness, withdrawal from social activities, changes in appetite or sleep patterns, and expressions of hopelessness or worry should be taken seriously.

These symptoms can indicate underlying conditions such as depression or anxiety, which can significantly affect their quality of life.

It's important to engage in open and empathetic conversations with our parents about their feelings and experiences, showing them that their mental health is a priority and that they are not alone in their struggles.

Seeking professional help is a vital step in managing mental health issues. Therapists and counselors specialized in geriatric psychology can provide our parents with the tools and strategies they need to cope with their emotions and challenges. These professionals can offer a safe space for our parents to express their feelings and work through their issues. Therapy can be particularly beneficial in helping them navigate the complexities of aging, offering support and guidance tailored to their unique experiences.

In addition to professional help, incorporating **mindfulness and relaxation practices** into our parents' routine can offer significant benefits. Practices such as mindfulness meditation, yoga, and deep-breathing exercises can help reduce stress, improve emotional regulation, and enhance overall mental well-being. These practices encourage a focus on the present moment, helping to alleviate worries about the past or future and fostering a sense of peace and contentment. Yoga, with its combination of physical postures, breathing techniques, and meditation, can be especially beneficial for the elderly, offering a holistic approach to well-being that encompasses both physical and mental health.

Cultivating a sense of inner peace and resilience is particularly important in countering the stresses associated with aging. By encouraging our parents to engage in mindfulness and relaxation practices, we can help them build a foundation of mental and emotional strength that supports them through the challenges of their golden years. These practices, along with professional support and a proactive approach to mental health, can empower our parents to lead more fulfilling, peaceful, and joyful lives, even as they face the complexities of aging.

Conclusion

Supporting the social and emotional well-being of our aging parents is a multifaceted endeavor that requires empathy, patience, and creativity. By understanding the nuances of their emotional needs, actively promoting social engagement and cognitive stimulation we can significantly impact their overall happiness and quality of life.

This chapter underscores the importance of a holistic approach to eldercare, one that cherishes and nurtures the heart and mind as much as the body.

Overview of Part IV
Case Studies and Resources

Executive Summary

Part IV, "Case Studies and Resources," serves as a practical supplement to the theoretical and strategic frameworks discussed earlier. This section aims to bring the concepts to life through real-world examples and provide you with a curated list of resources to aid in your eldercare journey.

Key Points:

1. **Real-Life Scenarios**

This chapter presents case studies that cover a range of eldercare situations, from

managing care from another country to dealing with dementia. These stories offer valuable insights and actionable takeaways.

2. **Resource Guide**

A comprehensive list of useful apps, websites, agencies, and organizations that can assist you in various aspects of eldercare. This guide serves as a quick reference for when you need expert help.

Learning Objectives:

- Gain practical insights into the complexities of eldercare through real-world case studies.
- Become familiar with a variety of resources that can assist you in managing eldercare more effectively.
- Learn how to apply theoretical knowledge in real-life scenarios for better decision-making.

Action Plan:

1. **Case Study Analysis**

Read through the case studies and identify the strategies and solutions that could

be applicable to your situation. Take notes for future reference.

2. Resource Compilation

Go through the resource guide and bookmark or save the resources that are most

relevant to your needs. Consider creating a digital folder for easy access.

3. Consult Experts

Use the resource guide to identify experts or organizations that can assist you. Schedule consultations or informational interviews to gather more personalized advice.

4. Family Briefing

Share the insights gained from the case studies and resources with family members involved in eldercare. Discuss how these can be integrated into your existing care plan.

5. Trial and Feedback

Implement some of the strategies or tools you've learned from the case studies or

resource guide on a trial basis. Gather feedback from your parent and care team to assess effectiveness.

6. Review and Update

After a trial period, review the outcomes and make necessary adjustments to your care plan. Keep the book and resource guide handy for ongoing reference and updates.

By following this action plan, you'll be better equipped to navigate the practical aspects of eldercare, armed with real-world examples and a robust set of resources. This section serves as a valuable toolkit for implementing and refining your eldercare strategies.

Chapter 16:
Case Studies

As Adult Children of Aging Parents (ACAPs), navigating the complexities of eldercare can be a daunting task, especially when faced with unique challenges like managing care from a distance or coordinating community care for a parent with dementia.

Executive Summary

This chapter aims to offer guidance and support to ACAPs through relatable and instructive case studies. These studies illustrate common challenges in eldercare and demonstrate effective strategies for managing these situations. The chapter also includes a resource guide to further aid ACAPs in finding the support and information they need.

In the heart of a small, close-knit community, the Johnson family faced the daunting journey of dementia care for their beloved matriarch, Mary. Mary, once the cornerstone of family gatherings and a vibrant storyteller, began showing signs of dementia, transforming the family's dynamic and challenging their resilience. The diagnosis brought not only emotional turmoil but also the pressing need to navigate the complexities of her evolving care requirements.

Case Study 1

Background:

The onset of Mary's condition was gradual, her once-sharp memory beginning to fray at the edges, leading to moments of confusion and distress. The realization that she could no longer live independently was a turning point for the Johnsons, prompting them to explore the labyrinth of care options available within their community. The task was formidable, with each family member grappling with their own emotions while striving to ensure Mary's dignity and quality of life.

Collaborative Approach:

Embracing a collaborative spirit, the Johnsons divided responsibilities according to each member's strengths and availability. John, the eldest son, took charge of researching and coordinating community resources, discovering an adult day care center that offered activities tailored to individuals with dementia.

This center became a haven for Mary, where she engaged in music therapy and painting, activities that reignited sparks of her former self. Sarah, a nurse by profession and Mary's granddaughter, coordinated with home health aides to ensure Mary's safety and comfort on days she spent at home.

The family also found solace and support in a local dementia support group, a community of families navigating similar paths, sharing strategies, and offering shoulders to lean on.

Outcome and Learnings:

The impact of these concerted efforts was profound. Mary's days were filled with engaging activities, reducing the frequency of her distress and confusion. The support group provided the family with coping strategies, making them feel less isolated in their struggles. Most importantly, the burden of care was distributed, alleviating individual stress and fostering a renewed sense of unity and purpose within the family.

Through their journey, the Johnsons learned the importance of community in dementia care—a network of resources and shared experiences that can lighten the load and brighten the darker paths of caregiving.

This case study underscores the vital role of collaborative approaches and community resources in managing dementia care. It highlights that while the journey may be fraught with challenges, the collective efforts of family and community can provide a scaffold of support, ensuring the well-being of both the caregiver and the cared-for.

For ACAPs embarking on similar journeys, the Johnsons' story serves as a beacon, illustrating that with compassion, collaboration, and community support, families can navigate the complexities of dementia care.

Case Study 2

The Carter family is caregiving for their aging father, Thomas, were tangled with complexity and strained relationships, particularly between two siblings,

Emily and Claire. Emily, the primary caregiver, navigated the daily challenges of managing Thomas's escalating health needs with dedication and love. Claire, however, remained distant, offering minimal assistance and often criticizing Emily's decisions, despite her limited involvement. This discord was further exacerbated by Claire's insistence on controlling a significant portion of their parents' finances, a point of contention that cast a shadow over family dynamics.

Background:

Thomas Carter, a widower with advancing Parkinson's disease, required increasing levels of care, a responsibility that fell largely on Emily's shoulders. As his condition deteriorated, so too did the relationship between Emily and Claire. Claire's visits were infrequent, and when she did appear, her presence was marked by hostility and criticism, leaving Emily feeling undervalued and overwhelmed. The tension reached a boiling point over discussions about the allocation of their father's savings, with Claire demanding a disproportionate share, despite her minimal contribution to his care.

Conflict and Resolution:

The ongoing conflict threatened to fracture the family, prompting Emily to seek a resolution that preserved their father's well-being and mended the strained sibling relationship. The solution came through the intervention of a family mediator, skilled in navigating such delicate situations. The mediator facilitated a series of discussions that encouraged open communication, empathy, and understanding among all family members.

In these sessions, Emily expressed the physical and emotional toll of caregiving, outlining the specific needs of their father and the associated costs. Claire was encouraged to share her perspective, revealing underlying feelings of guilt and inadequacy for not being more involved in her father's care. This honest exchange opened the door to a deeper understanding between the sisters.

Outcome and Learnings:

The breakthrough came when the mediator proposed a structured care plan that included both sisters, redistributing the caregiving responsibilities and financial management in a way that acknowledged Emily's primary role while actively involving Claire in their father's life. Claire agreed to take on specific tasks, such as managing medical appointments and contributing to financial planning, roles that leveraged her strengths and allowed her to be more involved without overstepping into Emily's primary caregiving duties.

The mediator helped them establish a fair financial agreement that reflected their contributions and responsibilities, ensuring Thomas's care needs were met without undue financial burden on Emily. This agreement also included setting aside funds for their father's future needs, with both sisters having equal input into the management of these resources.

Conclusion

The mediation process brought Emily and Claire closer, transforming their conflict into collaboration. It underscored the importance of open communication, empathy, and structured planning in resolving family caregiving disputes. Thomas benefited from a more unified family support system, while Emily and Claire learned to appreciate each other's contributions and limitations. This case study exemplifies how conflict, even in its most entrenched form, can be a catalyst for growth, understanding, and stronger family bonds when approached with openness, willingness to understand, and professional guidance.

Connect With Walt Kasmir, PhD

With a warm heart and a deep understanding of the intricate journey of aging, I bring a unique perspective to Eldercare Coaching. My path in this field is not just professional, but deeply personal. As a gerontologist, I've dedicated my life to understanding the aging process, offering guidance and support to hundreds of families navigating this complex and often emotional terrain.

My expertise is rooted in both academic knowledge and real-world experience. I've walked this path myself. The gradual decline of my own parents, especially the heart-wrenching progression of Alzheimer's disease, has given me firsthand insight into the struggles many families face. This personal journey has not only deepened my empathy but has also fueled my passion for supporting others through similar experiences.

I believe in a holistic approach to eldercare, one that honors the dignity and individuality of each aging individual while providing their families with the understanding and tools they need to make informed, compassionate decisions. My mission is to be a guiding light in what can often be a dark and confusing time, offering a blend of wisdom, empathy, and practical strategies to those who are grappling with the complexities of caring for aging loved ones.

Read My Other Books...
Gain Exclusive Access To Me For Consultations...
Join Social Live Streams and Webinars...
Book Me To Speak...
Apply For Or Appeal For Your Social Security Disability...
Just visit me at **DrWaltKasmir.com**[1]. Together, we can navigate this journey with grace and understanding, creating a path that respects the needs of both the elderly and their families.

Oh, one more thing. If you've benefited from this book, please leave me a 5-Star Review.

Blessings!

---

1. http://DrWaltKasmir.com

Appendix A:

Medicare and Medicaid terms tailored for Adult Children of Aging Parents (ACAPs).

This glossary is designed to provide a broader understanding of the key terms and concepts you might encounter as you navigate through the complexities of eldercare.

Advantage Plans (Medicare Part C): Private health plans that are Medicare-approved and provide all Part A and Part B services and may include Part D (prescription drug coverage).

Benefit Period: The way Medicare measures your use of hospital and skilled nursing facility (SNF) also know as rehabilitation services.

Coverage Gap (Donut Hole): A temporary limit on what most Medicare Part D Prescription Drug Plans or Medicare Advantage Prescription Drug plans will cover for drugs.

Dual Eligible: Individuals who are entitled to Medicare Part A and/or Part B and are eligible for some form of Medicaid benefit.

Extra Help: A Medicare program to help people with limited income and resources pay Medicare prescription drug program costs, like premiums, deductibles, and coinsurance.

Fee-for-Service (FFS): The traditional healthcare payment system under which doctors and other healthcare providers are paid for each service performed.

Guaranteed Issue Rights: Rights you have in certain situations when insurance companies must offer you certain Medigap policies.

Health Maintenance Organization (HMO): A type of health insurance plan that usually limits coverage to care from doctors who work for or contract with the HMO.

Inpatient Care: Care you receive when you're admitted to a hospital or skilled nursing facility.

Justification of Coverage: A document or statement that explains why a particular medical procedure or service was necessary and covered.

Lifetime Reserve Days: In Medicare Part A, these are a set number of days that Medicare will pay for when you're in a hospital for more than 90 days during a benefit period.

Medicare: Federal health insurance program for people who are 65 or older, certain younger people with disabilities, and people with End-Stage Renal Disease.

Medicare Part D and Medicare Advantage plans are both options to help with the cost of prescription drugs, but they work in different ways.

Medicare Part D: is a standalone prescription drug plan (PDP) that can be added to Original Medicare (Parts A and B) or a Medicare Supplement Insurance (Medigap) plan. These plans are offered by private insurance companies approved by Medicare. Part D plans vary in cost and coverage, but they all provide a formulary, which is a list of drugs they cover, and have different tiers with different costs for each drug.

Medicare Advantage (Part C): is an all-in-one alternative to Original Medicare (Parts A and B). These plans are also offered by private insurance companies approved by Medicare. Medicare Advantage plans must cover everything Original Medicare covers, and most include prescription drug coverage (Part D). They often have additional benefits, like vision, dental, and fitness programs, and usually have a network of doctors and hospitals you must use.

Choosing between the two depends on your individual needs and preferences. If you value flexibility in choosing your doctors and hospitals and want to keep Original Medicare, you might choose a Part D plan. If you prefer the convenience of having all your coverage under one plan and are comfortable with a network of providers, a Medicare Advantage plan might be a better fit.

Non-Participating Provider: A medical provider who doesn't accept Medicare assignment but can still choose to accept Medicare patients.

Original Medicare: Refers to Medicare Part A (Hospital Insurance) and Part B (Medical Insurance).

Preferred Provider Organization (PPO): A type of health plan that contracts with medical providers, such as hospitals and doctors, to create a network of participating providers.

Qualified Medicare Beneficiary (QMB) Program: A Medicaid program that helps very low-income seniors and other qualified individuals with Medicare premiums, deductibles, and coinsurance costs.

Referral: A written order from your primary care doctor for you to see a specialist or get certain medical services in an HMO.

Special Needs Plan (SNP): A specialized type of Medicare Advantage plan that provides targeted care and covers benefits, providers, and drug formularies for specific groups of people.

Tricare: Health care program for uniformed service members, retirees, and their families.

Underwriting: The process by which an insurance company determines whether to accept a risk and, if so, what amount of coverage and premium rate to offer.

Voluntary Enrollment: The process by which individuals choose to enroll in a

Appendix B:

Glossary of medical conditions that are relevant to Adult Children Of Aging Parents (ACAPs).
This glossary includes the diagnosis, treatment, and relevance to ACAPs for each condition, providing a valuable resource for navigating eldercare challenges.

Alzheimer's Disease

- **Etiology:** The most common cause of dementia, characterized by the accumulation of amyloid plaques and tau tangles in the brain.
- **Diagnosis:** Alzheimer's disease is diagnosed through a comprehensive evaluation that may include patient history, cognitive tests, neurological exams, and brain imaging (MRI or CT scans) to rule out other causes of dementia symptoms.
- **Prognosis:** Progressive decline in cognitive and functional abilities. Average life expectancy after diagnosis is 4 to 8 years, but individuals can live up to 20 years.
- **Signs and Symptoms:** Memory loss that disrupts daily life, challenges in planning or solving problems, difficulty completing familiar tasks, confusion with time or place, trouble understanding visual images and spatial relationships, new problems with words in speaking or writing, misplacing things and losing the ability to retrace steps, decreased or poor judgment, withdrawal from work or social activities, changes in mood and personality.
- **Treatment:** There is no cure for Alzheimer's, but treatments can temporarily slow the worsening of symptoms. Medications for memory loss and other cognitive symptoms include cholinesterase inhibitors and memantine. Supportive therapies like cognitive stimulation and lifestyle changes are also recommended.
- **ACAP Relevance:** ACAPs need to focus on creating a safe and supportive environment, managing medications, and providing

emotional support. Legal and financial planning are also important.

Vascular Dementia

- **Etiology:** Caused by conditions that block or reduce blood flow to the brain, leading to brain damage.
- **Diagnosis:** Imaging studies such as MRI and CT scans can detect changes in the brain's blood vessels.
- **Prognosis:** The progression can be slowed with treatment but varies greatly among individuals. The course is often stepwise rather than gradual.
- **Signs and Symptoms:** Manifests through memory lapses, difficulty in planning and solving problems, and mood swings. Physical symptoms may include weakness on one side of the body, problems with coordination, and urinary incontinence.

Lewy Body Dementia

- **Etiology:** Characterized by abnormal deposits of a protein called alpha-synuclein in the brain.
- **Diagnosis:** Based on clinical symptoms, with supportive evidence from neuroimaging.
- **Prognosis:** Progressive disease with an average duration from onset to death of 5 to 8 years.
- **Signs and Symptoms:** Lewy Body Dementia is characterized by fluctuating cognitive abilities, vivid visual hallucinations, and motor symptoms akin to Parkinson's disease, such as rigidity and tremors. Individuals may experience sleep disturbances, including acting out dreams, and significant changes in alertness and attention. Recognizing these symptoms early is crucial for managing care and improving the life quality of those affected.
- **Treatment:** Symptomatic treatment for cognitive symptoms and psychosis. Medications used in Parkinson's disease can help with movement symptoms.
- **ACAP Relevance:** Involves understanding and managing complex

symptoms like fluctuations in cognitive status, visual hallucinations, and Parkinsonian movement features. Safety and supportive care are paramount.

Frontotemporal Dementia

- **Etiology:** Involves damage to neurons in the frontal and temporal lobes of the brain. Can be genetic in some cases.
- **Diagnosis:** Assessment includes clinical evaluation, genetic testing, and brain imaging.
- **Prognosis:** Progressive and rapid decline compared to other dementias. Life expectancy is approximately 7 to 13 years after symptoms begin.
- **Signs and Symptoms:** Frontotemporal Dementia (FTD) presents with marked changes in personality and behavior, including impulsivity, apathy, and inappropriate social conduct, reflecting its impact on the brain's frontal and temporal lobes. Language difficulties are also common, ranging from speaking less to having trouble understanding or producing speech. Early detection is key, as these symptoms can significantly affect relationships and daily functioning, requiring targeted support and management strategies.
- **Treatment:** No specific treatment. Management focuses on symptom relief, including medications for behavior problems and speech therapy.
- **ACAP Relevance:** Care strategies include managing behavioral symptoms, communication aids, and creating a structured environment. Emotional support for the family is also crucial.

Mixed Dementia

- **Etiology:** A condition in which changes representing more than one type of dementia occur simultaneously in the brain.
- **Diagnosis:** Often diagnosed posthumously. Clinically, it presents with symptoms of more than one dementia type.
- **Prognosis:** Depends on the types of dementias present and their

progression.

- **Signs and Symptoms:** Mixed dementia, which involves the simultaneous presence of Alzheimer's and another type of dementia, often displays a combination of symptoms, including memory loss, difficulty with problem-solving, and changes in mood and behavior. Individuals may also experience symptoms specific to the co-occurring type of dementia, such as vascular dementia's physical symptoms or Lewy body dementia's visual hallucinations. The overlapping symptoms can complicate diagnosis and management, emphasizing the importance of comprehensive care approaches tailored to the individual's diverse needs.
- **Treatment:** Symptomatic treatment based on the types of dementia diagnosed and the most prominent symptoms.
- **ACAP Relevance:** Requires a versatile care approach tailored to the mixed symptoms experienced by the individual. Supportive care, environmental adjustments, and comprehensive medical management are key.

Age-Related Macular Degeneration (AMD)

- **Diagnosis:** Comprehensive eye exams that include visual acuity tests and dilated eye exams. Advanced AMD may be diagnosed through fluorescein angiography and optical coherence tomography.
- **Signs and Symptoms:** Blurred vision, dark, blurry areas in the center of vision, and colors that seem less bright.
- **Treatment:** While there's no cure for early AMD, progression can be slowed with specific high-dose vitamins and minerals. For late AMD, treatments include anti-VEGF injections, laser therapy, and photodynamic therapy.
- **ACAP Relevance:** ACAPs can help by ensuring their parents receive regular eye exams to catch AMD early, assisting with treatment adherence, and making living adjustments to accommodate vision loss.

Arthritis

Arthritis encompasses various conditions characterized by inflammation and pain in the joints, impacting mobility and quality of life.

Arthritis is not a single disease; it includes over 100 different conditions. The most common types affecting the elderly include:

- **Osteoarthritis (OA):** The most common form, resulting from wear and tear of the cartilage that cushions the ends of bones in the joints.

- **Rheumatoid Arthritis (RA):** An autoimmune disease where the immune system attacks the joints, leading to inflammation and joint damage.

- **Gout:** Caused by the crystallization of uric acid within the joints, leading to sudden and severe episodes of pain and swelling.

Diagnosis: The diagnosis of arthritis involves a combination of clinical examination and diagnostic tests. A healthcare provider will look for joint swelling, redness, warmth, and mobility. X-rays, MRI, and ultrasound can help visualize joint damage, inflammation, and fluid accumulation. Certain blood tests can identify markers of inflammation or antibodies associated with specific types of arthritis, like RA.

Signs and Symptoms: While symptoms can vary depending on the type of arthritis, common indicators include (1) joint pain, which varies in severity and may worsen after activity, (2) stiffness especially noticeable upon waking up or after periods of inactivity, (3) swelling and redness around the joints, making them tender to the touch, and (4) decreased range of motion, making daily activities challenging.

Treatment: Treatment for arthritis aims to reduce symptoms and improve quality of life. Options include (1) pain relievers (analgesics), non-steroidal anti-inflammatory drugs (NSAIDs), and disease-modifying antirheumatic drugs (DMARDs) for RA, (2) physical therapy can help improve joint function through exercises that strengthen the muscles around the joints, improve flexibility, and reduce pain, (3) weight management, a healthy diet, and regular exercise can alleviate symptoms and improve overall health, and (4) in severe cases, joint repair, replacement, or fusion surgeries may be considered.

Relevance to ACAPs:

Understanding arthritis is crucial for ACAPs as they may need to assist their aging parents with:

- **Daily Activities:** Modifying tasks to make them easier and less painful.
- **Medical Appointments:** Coordinating visits to healthcare providers for ongoing management and treatment adjustments.
- **Home Safety:** Implementing modifications to reduce fall risk and accommodate limited mobility.
- **Emotional Support:** Coping with the frustration and depression that can accompany chronic pain and mobility issues.

Atrial Fibrillation

- **Diagnosis:** Diagnosed through an electrocardiogram (ECG) which records the heart's electrical activity.
- **Signs and Symptoms:** Irregular and rapid heart rate, heart palpitations, fatigue, dizziness, shortness of breath, and weakness.
- **Treatment:** Treatment aims to control the heart rate, prevent blood clots, and reduce stroke risk. It can include medications, electrical cardioversion, catheter ablation, and surgery.

- **ACAP Relevance:** ACAPs need to understand the importance of regular monitoring, medication adherence, and lifestyle adjustments to manage this condition effectively.

Chronic Obstructive Pulmonary Disease (COPD)

- **Diagnosis:** COPD is diagnosed through a review of symptoms, a physical exam, and pulmonary function tests, including spirometry, which measures the amount and speed of air a person can inhale and exhale.

- **Signs and Symptoms:** Persistent respiratory symptoms like dyspnea (difficulty breathing), chronic cough, frequent clearing of the throat, and wheezing. Symptoms often worsen over time.
- **Treatment:** While there's no cure for COPD, treatments can manage symptoms. These include smoking cessation, inhaled bronchodilators, steroids, pulmonary rehabilitation, and oxygen therapy.
- **ACAP Relevance:** Caregivers may need to assist with smoking cessation programs, medication management, and the arrangement of home oxygen supplies. Understanding how to recognize exacerbations and when to seek emergency care is crucial.

Compromised Immune Systems

- **Diagnosis:** Diagnosed through blood tests that measure white blood cell counts, immune system markers, and the presence of autoantibodies. Specialized tests may assess the response to vaccines or infections.
- **Signs and Symptoms:** Increased susceptibility to infections, slow healing wounds, fatigue, and possibly recurring fever or illness.
- **Treatment:** Treatment strategies may include medication to boost the immune system, antibiotics to prevent infections, and vaccinations. Lifestyle changes such as a nutritious diet, adequate sleep, and stress reduction are also important.
- **ACAP Relevance:** ACAPs should ensure a clean and safe living environment for their parents, facilitate regular health check-ups, and encourage a healthy lifestyle to support immune function. Being vigilant about signs of infection or illness is crucial for early intervention.

Breast Cancer

- **Diagnosis:** Mammograms are the primary screening tool, with ultrasounds and biopsies used for further investigation if abnormalities are detected.

- **Signs and Symptoms:** A lump in the breast or underarm, changes in breast size or shape, skin dimpling, nipple discharge other than breast milk, or pain in any area of the breast.

- **Treatment:** Treatment may include surgery, radiation therapy, chemotherapy, hormone therapy, or targeted therapy, depending on the cancer stage and type.

- **ACAP Relevance:** ACAPs may assist in managing treatment schedules, providing transportation to appointments, and offering emotional support. Understanding the potential side effects of treatments can help in providing better care.

Colorectal Cancer

- **Diagnosis:** Colonoscopy is the primary diagnostic and screening tool, with biopsies taken of any suspicious areas.

- **Signs and Symptoms:** Changes in bowel habits, rectal bleeding or blood in the stool, persistent abdominal discomfort, weakness, or fatigue.

- **Treatment:** Depending on the stage, treatments include surgery, radiation therapy, chemotherapy, and targeted therapy.

- **ACAP Relevance:** ACAPs can help by encouraging regular screenings, supporting their parents through treatment, and helping manage dietary and lifestyle changes post-diagnosis.

Lung Cancer

- **Diagnosis:** Diagnosed through imaging tests like CT scans and confirmed by biopsy.

- **Signs and Symptoms:** Persistent cough, coughing up blood, chest pain, shortness of breath, weight loss, and fatigue.

- **Treatment:** Treatment may involve surgery, radiation, chemotherapy, targeted therapy, or a combination of these, depending on the cancer type and stage.

- **ACAP Relevance:** ACAPs play a crucial role in supporting their parents through the treatment process, from decision-making to managing side effects and ensuring emotional and physical comfort.

Prostate Cancer

- **Diagnosis:** Screening includes prostate-specific antigen (PSA) blood tests and digital rectal exams. Biopsies are performed if abnormalities are suspected.

- **Signs and Symptoms:** Difficulty urinating, decreased force in the stream of urine, blood in urine, pelvic discomfort, bone pain, and erectile dysfunction.

- **Treatment:** Options include watchful waiting, surgery, radiation therapy, hormone therapy, chemotherapy, and biologic therapy, depending on the cancer's aggressiveness and stage.

- **ACAP Relevance:** ACAPs may need to discuss treatment options with their parents, ensuring they understand the potential benefits and side effects.

- **Congestive Heart Failure (CHF)**

- **Diagnosis:** Diagnosed via patient history, physical exam, and tests like echocardiograms, MRIs, or blood tests.
- **Treatment:** Treatment focuses on managing symptoms through medication, lifestyle changes, and in severe cases, surgery or devices.
- **ACAP Relevance:** Caregivers should understand symptom management, emergency signs, and the importance of dietary and fluid restrictions.

Depression

- **Diagnosis:** Diagnosed based on patient history, self-reported symptoms, and a physical examination to rule out other causes. Screening tools and clinical interviews may be used.
- **Signs and Symptoms:** Persistent sadness, loss of interest in activities, significant weight loss or gain, sleep disturbances, energy loss, feelings of worthlessness, and thoughts of death or suicide.
- **Treatment:** Treatment includes antidepressant medications, psychotherapy, lifestyle changes, and support groups.
- **ACAP Relevance:** ACAPs play a critical role in recognizing signs of depression in their parents, encouraging treatment, providing emotional support, and monitoring for any treatment side effects.

Diabetes

- **Diagnosis:** Blood tests such as the fasting plasma glucose test or the A1C test.
- **Treatment:** Management includes medication, insulin therapy, diet changes, and regular exercise.
- **ACAP Relevance:** They may help manage blood sugar monitoring, diet, and medication schedules.

Osteoporosis

- **Diagnosis:** Bone density scans assess bone health and risk of fractures.
- **Treatment:** Includes calcium and vitamin D supplementation, medications to slow bone loss, and exercise to strengthen bones.
- **ACAP Relevance:** Caregivers need to be vigilant about fall prevention and ensure that homes are safe for elderly parents with frail bones.

Parkinson's Disease

- **Diagnosis:** Diagnosed based on medical history, symptoms, and neurological examinations; no specific test exists.

- **Treatment:** Treatment may include medication, physical therapy, and in advanced cases, surgical options like deep brain stimulation.
- **ACAP Relevance:** ACAPs play a key role in providing emotional support, managing medication schedules, and adapting living environments.

Stroke or Cardiovascular Accident (CVA)

- **Diagnosis:** Immediate imaging tests like CT scans or MRIs to determine the type of stroke and its location.
- **Treatment:** Treatments vary by type but may include clot-busting drugs, surgery, and rehabilitation.
- **ACAP Relevance:** Post-stroke care often requires ACAPs to coordinate rehabilitation, speech therapy, and modifications for any long-term disabilities.

Urinary Incontinence

- **Diagnosis:** Diagnosed through medical history, bladder diary, and physical exams.
- **Treatment:** Treatment options include pelvic floor exercises, medications, and sometimes surgery.
- **ACAP Relevance:** ACAPs may assist in managing treatment plans and adapting daily routines and home environments to manage incontinence effectively.

For ACAPs, understanding these medical conditions is crucial for providing the necessary support, care, and advocacy for their aging parents. It involves being informed about the latest treatments, facilitating access to quality healthcare, and offering the emotional and physical support needed during challenging times.

Epilogue:
A Beacon of Hope

The later years of our loved ones hold a melody that resonates with the depth of our shared experiences, the richness of their wisdom, and the vulnerability of their needs. "The Artistry of Eldercare: A Guide for ACAPs" has been a journey through the harmonious blend of practical advice and compassionate insights, aiming to elevate the act of caregiving from a duty to an art form. As we close this chapter, let's reflect on the transformative power of this guide, not just for Adult Children of Aging Parents (ACAPs) but for all who find themselves intertwined in the delicate dance of eldercare.

This guide has painted a vivid picture of eldercare, illustrating not only the challenges but also the profound joys and opportunities for growth it presents. For ACAPs, it has served as a palette of strategies, emotions, and understanding, enabling them to craft a caregiving experience that honors the dignity, history, and humanity of their aging loved ones. For supporters, community groups, and faith-based leaders, it has offered insights into creating a support network that views eldercare as a shared responsibility and privilege. Imagine a world where eldercare is recognized for what it truly is—an art form that requires patience, skill, and above all, love. A world where communities come together to ensure that the twilight years of our elders are filled with warmth, respect, and joy. This guide invites us to envision and work towards this reality, empowering us with the knowledge and compassion needed to make a meaningful difference in the lives of those we care for.

As we move forward, let this guide inspire you to take action. If you're an ACAP, let it be your companion and counselor as you navigate the complexities of caregiving. For community and faith-based leaders, let it serve as a blueprint for building programs and initiatives that support eldercare. Together, we can transform the landscape of aging, ensuring that every elder is cared for with the love, respect, and dignity they deserve.

In closing, "The Artistry of Eldercare" is more than a guide—it's a call to embrace the beauty, challenges, and responsibilities of caring for our aging loved ones. It's an invitation to create a masterpiece of compassion and support that will stand as a testament to our collective capacity for love and care. Let us answer this call with open hearts and willing hands, crafting a future where eldercare is recognized as one of the highest forms of artistry.

Blessings!

About the Author

I bring a unique perspective to Eldercare Coaching. My path in this field is not just professional, but deeply personal. As a gerontologist, I've dedicated my life to understanding the aging process, offering guidance and support to hundreds of families navigating this complex and often emotional terrain.

My expertise is rooted in both academic knowledge and real-world experience. The challenges faced by Adult Children With Aging Parents are close to my heart, as I've walked this path myself. The gradual decline of my own parents, especially the heart-wrenching progression of Alzheimer's disease, has given me firsthand insight into the struggles many families face. This personal journey has not only deepened my empathy but has also fueled my passion for supporting others through similar experiences.

I believe in a holistic approach to eldercare, one that honors the dignity and individuality of each aging individual while providing their families with the understanding and tools they need to make informed, compassionate decisions.

My mission is to be a guiding light in what can often be a dark and confusing time, offering a blend of wisdom, empathy, and practical strategies to those who are grappling with the complexities of caring for aging loved ones.

Together, we can navigate this journey with grace and understanding, creating a path that respects the needs of both the elderly and their families.
Read more at https://DrWaltKasmir.com.

www.ingramcontent.com/pod-product-compliance
Lightning Source LLC
Chambersburg PA
CBHW052007150726
47999CB00004B/1558